TEEING OFF

ALSO BY KEN BOWDEN

Golf Gazetteer, 1969, 1973
   With Gay Brewer
Score Better Than You Swing, 1971
   With John Jacobs
Play Better Golf, 1969
Practical Golf, 1972 and four re-publications
John Jacobs Analyses Golf's Superstars, 1974
The Golf Swing Simplified, 1993
   With Jack Nicklaus
Golf My Way, 1974; updated edition 2005
Jack Nicklaus' Lesson Tee, 1976
On and Off the Fairway, 1978
Play Better Golf: The Swing from A–Z, 1980
Playing Lessons, 1981
Play Better Golf: The Short Game and Scoring, 1981
The Full Swing, 1982
Play Better Golf: Short Cuts to Lower Scores, 1983
My Most Memorable Shots in the Majors, 1988
Jack Nicklaus Golf Handbook, 1996
My Story, 1997; updated edition 2007
My Golden Lessons, 2002

TEEING OFF

Players, Techniques, Characters,
Experiences, & Reflections from a
Lifetime Inside Golf

KEN BOWDEN

FOREWORD BY JACK NICKLAUS

TRIUMPH
BOOKS

Library of Congress Cataloging-in-Publication Data

Bowden, Ken.
   Teeing off : players, techniques, characters, experiences, and reflections from a lifetime inside golf / Ken Bowden; foreword by Jack Nicklaus.
      p. cm.
   ISBN-13: 978-1-60078-075-2
   ISBN-10: 1-60078-075-X
   1. Golf. 2. Golfers. 3. Bowden, Ken. I. Title.
   GV965.B63 2008
   796.352–dc22

                                    2008000422

This book is available in quantity at special discounts for your group or organization. For further information, contact:

Triumph Books
542 South Dearborn Street, Suite 750
Chicago, Illinois 60605
(312) 939-3330
Fax (312) 663-3557

Printed in U.S.A.
ISBN: 978-1-60078-075-2
Design, editorial, and page production by Prologue Publishing Services, LLC.

FOR JEAN
who shared so much of the journey,
with boundless love, care, and help

GOFFERS

It is a well knowne fact that Goffers are a tribe aparte.

Thru playing Goff unceasingly their very natures change, and they become tacurne, sullen, peevish and irritable!

They speake, eat, drink, sleepe and jabber Goff, forgetting their chattels and infants and spend monies only on balls, clubbs or a majic drink called wiski.

The clubb makers and wiski-sellers make enormous fortunes, while the Goffers families are in great famine.

These Goffers have been knowne to rise with the lark to play Goff, and continue throughout the daylite hours only stopping for short tymes and wiski.

Such are the very odd ways of goffers.

From an edict banning golf in Scotland by Decree of King James IV in 1457 because, "It is Agin the Common Goode of the Realme and Defense Thereof."

CONTENTS

Foreword by Jack Nicklaus...xiii

Introduction...xv

Part I: Players

1: My Greatest of the Greats 3

2: Interviewing the "Wee Ice Mon".....................................12

3: Hogan at Work..19

4: The Nicklaus Psyche—The Man 22

5: The Nicklaus Psyche—The Golfer 26

6: The Bear Up Close and Personal 30

7: "Only a Game"...34

8: Golf's Ultimate Pro 37

9: The Greatest Round Ever Played?....................................41

10: Golf's First Great Non-Brit or Yankee...........................45

11: Señor Magical Mercurial 49

12: "It Was Genius" 52

13: Good for the Kidneys...54

14: Mr. Generosity 56

15: No More Great Rivalries?..58

16: "The Stupid Nature of the Idiot Game"............................60

17: Major Championship Quiz................................62

Part II: Technique

18: At Last!..67

19: A Form of Masochism!................................68

20: Searching for Golf's Holy Grail........................69

21: Working with Britain's "Dr. Golf"....................71

22: "Mighty Mouse"..................................73

23: "One and Indivisible"............................76

24: The Secret....................................79

25: Published Instruction: Garbage or Gold?............81

26: "Once You've Had 'Em, You've Got 'Em!"............84

27: Great Pupils Sure Help............................85

28: My Best-Ever (Temporary!) Swing Fix................86

29: Power..88

30: Improving....................................90

31: On "Gimmes"..................................92

32: "It's Like Sex, Old Boy"........................94

33: Too Difficult?................................96

Part III: Characters

34: "Let the Bugger Go!"............................99

35: Stars: "Proximity Breeds Disenchantment"............105

36: A Literary Genius's Darker Side....................108

37: Working with Mr. Roberts........................112

38: "Like Stalin Ruled Russia"..117

39: Ultimate Devotion..121

40: Mr. Roberts Signs Off..123

41: Characters or Jackasses?...125

42: 007..130

43: Scottish Loopers..133

44: Churchill on Golf...136

45: "Well, If You Were to…"..137

46: "Just *Too* Damn Frustrating"..139

Part IV: Experiences

47: Whine at Your Peril...145

48: Touches of Scotland...147

49: Premonition...150

50: Memorial Highs…and Lows...152

51: Showbiz Golf..156

52: Coming to America...172

53: Conning an English Rose..178

Part V: Reflections

54: "To Hell with 'Em!"...183

55: Absurd Penalties..186

56: Married to the Game...189

57: Golf's Battle of the Sexes..191

58: Treat 'Em Right..194

59: "Sandbaggers"...195

60: "Vanity" Handicaps 196

61: The Equality Quest 197

62: Racism in Golf 199

63: All About Money? 201

64: Dream Living? 202

65: Beware Politics 204

66: Golf Club Discipline 205

67: Carts 207

68: Masters Course Bad for Golf? 208

69: Overboard U.S. Open Setups—Boring! 210

70: Tour Golf's Darker Sides 213

71: "Team Spirit" 215

72: Media Mauling 217

73: "Lip-Flap" 220

74: Golfer Speak 222

75: The Joys of "Spectating" 223

76: Equipment Cost and Confusion 225

77: Bomb and Gouging versus Powder-Puffing 227

78: Unimportant 231

79: No D-Average Golfers Allowed 232

80: Why So Popular 233

Index 237

FOREWORD

BY JACK NICKLAUS

Although our paths had crossed earlier in my career, I truly got to know
Ken Bowden in the early 1970s after he joined a small group I had
put together to help handle my business affairs.

By that time, I was about a decade into my professional golf career,
and Ken was an established writer and editor. He had cofounded and
edited what quickly became—and remains—Great Britain's top golf
magazine. That was followed by a spell as editorial chief of America's
Golf Digest, a publication to which he brought me aboard and with
which I still enjoy a relationship today.

As I write almost 40 years after our first business association, we have
collaborated on thousands of newspaper and magazine articles, in addition to a dozen books about the game of golf. Ken also helped direct the
creation of my instructional videos, plus numerous television shows
around the world, and assisted me in the early 1990s when I dabbled in
commentary for network golf tournament broadcasts. Ken, as well as his
wife, Jean, also provided critical support to my Memorial Tournament,
from its formative stages through its 32nd playing in 2006, in recognition
of which he was made an honorary life member of Muirfield Village Golf
Club. He was also selected by his peers as the recipient of the 2008
Memorial Golf Journalism Award.

Obviously, a relationship that works as happily and productively as
ours has for so long requires enthusiasm, ability, energy, compatibility,
and trust. I'm sure Ken agrees that we have enjoyed all of those qualities
and more to the fullest extent. As people who know me best are only too
aware, I have never been shy about speaking my mind, and not the least

important factor in our years of collaboration was Ken's readiness to do the same.

What also helped me tremendously were two qualities of Ken's that are critical to all relationships such as ours.

The first was his keen interest and enthusiasm for watching me play golf. My wife, Barbara, has been without question my number-one fan over the years, but Ken arguably flew and walked more miles to observe Jack Nicklaus at work than anyone outside my family. In fact, it came up in recent conversation that he has seen me compete in 10 countries, and that he missed watching in the flesh only two or three of my professional major championship victories.

The second significant quality Ken brought to our relationship was his knowledge of golf. Driven by a deep love of the game from an early age, Ken made himself as well-informed about virtually all elements of our common passion as anyone in his business. In addition, Ken was and remains a good player—from a plus-handicap in his prime to a single-digit golfer in his eighth decade. That was key when we needed to share insights about the technical aspects of the game and its techniques. In short, we spoke the same language.

Ken has always been a lively storyteller about his depth and breadth of experiences in golf, and particularly those containing some element of humor. Because of that, many friends of Ken's have long encouraged him to write a memoir. *Teeing Off* is not quite that in the dictionary sense of the word, but is rather—as its subtitle suggests—a collection of reminiscences and anecdotes from a lifetime of loving, playing, watching, and working around the game, mostly at its highest levels. The exception is the last of the book's five sections, in which Ken offers reflections and opinions about elements of golf that have especially caught his attention or triggered his concern. As mentioned before, Ken never shied away from speaking his mind!

Teeing Off seems to me to be a very different kind of golf book, particularly in its exceptionally wide range of subject matter. What is for sure is that you will know much more about the "inside" of the game when you have finished the book, and that it will make you think as well as laugh…sometimes at yourself.

INTRODUCTION

I plunged permanently into golf writing/editing late one night in a famous pub off London's Fleet Street, where I'd spent a well-lubricated evening with a man who owned the press that printed the British edition of *Readers' Digest*.

I'd freelanced some about the game while working full-time on other subjects for British newspapers and magazines. But this was the high dive.

The man's name was Charles Brett, and one of the first things he told me made me like him immediately. This was that, whenever he wanted a table at an overbooked elite British restaurant, he invariably got one by having his secretary preface his name with "Sir," thereby signifying that a knight of the realm would be honoring the joint with his presence. Tried it a time or two myself, and it worked great.

That evening, in the heart of Britain's newspaperland, I discovered five more things about Charles Brett.

One was that he owned a printing business in the southern part of England that had made him wealthy. Second, although never a really good player, he adored golf. Third, he shared my low opinion of Britain's weekly and monthly golf magazines of that period. Fourth, he had major printing-press time and capacity that he wanted to fill with publications in addition to *Readers' Digest*. Fifth, he could imbibe more gin and tonics and remain both standing and sentient than anyone else I knew!

A few (more sober) meetings later, we finalized launching a monthly magazine called *Golf World*, with Brett as founder/principal owner/publisher, myself as editor, a hotshot salesman lured as advertising chief from a lurid Sunday newspaper, and a gorgeous blonde called Jean Mackie, whom I later married, as everyone's Girl Friday.

I always suspected that the London offices we initially worked out of were chosen by Brett because the up-market bar of a characterful old Victorian pub, the Royal Albert, was only seconds away. Whatever, either over lunch or after hours—or both—it hosted more of our planning and idea-generating sessions than the office ever came close to doing.

The first edition of *Golf World* appeared in March of 1962. After some early bumpiness, the magazine succeeded surprisingly quickly for a new publication facing substantial competition, and our little team spent a happy six or so years making it into Europe's undisputed leader in the field.

But there then occurred a dispute over business's primary dispute-provoker worldwide: money. Whereupon, unhappy with the outcome, I abandoned ship to spend a couple of years in another golf-related endeavor fronted by John Jacobs, the doyen of British golf instructors, who, as my first contributor hire for *Golf World*, had become and remains a close friend.

Those years of editing *Golf World*, of course, immersed me in every element of the game throughout Europe, and eventually—thanks to a man to whom I will forever be indebted—also North America and much of the rest of the world. A brilliant if frequently maddeningly mercurial Chicagoan named William H. "Bill" Davis, he was the primary founder and for many years the overall chieftain of what was then and remains today golf's premier magazine, namely *Golf Digest*.

Bill and I met for the first time at the 1965 Ryder Cup at Britain's Royal Birkdale. Over dinner there, he told me he'd followed the progress of *Golf World* since its inception, and that what most impressed him about the magazine as it grew and evolved was it's "imaginative and highly instruction-oriented" editorial approach to the game. As we talked more, he asked me about the mechanics of the operation. By then, we'd moved offices south to Brett's home turf of Sussex and added a few more bodies, and I described how we put the "book" out each month while lunching leisurely most days in nearby pubs, then frequently vamoosing to play golf by mid-afternoon, the owner included.

Relative to that latter comment, knowing what I did about the American work ethic, I was a little surprised when, toward the end of our meal, Bill invited me to become *Golf Digest's* first European contributor. I accepted, wrote numerous pieces for the magazine, and from that graduated to crossing the pond each year to guest-edit an issue and help plan others.

As our relationship deepened with those enjoyable—and, as far as I know, successful—stints (no one told me one way or the other), Bill Davis seemed to become increasingly intrigued by my somewhat nonconformist outlook on life, by my 2-handicap golf game, and, perhaps most of all, by the number of story and other circulation-building ideas I endlessly pelted him with. The upshot of which was that, in seeking to upgrade *Digest* following its 1969 purchase by the New York Times Company, there came a day when he offered me the newly created position of editorial director.

Looking back on life, we all remember our biggest boo-boos, and—if only as a lesson to others in similar situations—permit me to digress about one of mine.

Having expressed strong interest in the job, it was arranged for me to spend a month or so in Connecticut, where the magazine's offices were then and still are based, serving what clearly would be a final trial period.

Representing the Times in the matter of my employment was a dapper vice president from the company's business side who, if everything else worked out, I had been told would negotiate terms with me. Accordingly, having apparently passed the test, and with my return to Britain imminent, the V.P. called and asked me to join him for lunch for that purpose at Sardi's, the famous restaurant handy to the Times's midtown headquarters. By then, of course, I'd thought long and hard on the subject, in addition to gleaning as much advice as possible from *Digest* employees to whom I'd become close.

Out came the lunch and, with our plates cleared, the V.P. pushed back his chair and said, "Okay, Kenny, down to business. Bill Davis tells me you're taking the job."

I indicated that was true, given only that my wife—the aforementioned gorgeous blonde—was comfortable with the move, to ascertain which Bill had already agreed to *Digest* hosting us for a brief U.S. vacation for the purpose of introducing her to a country she had never visited (*see page 178*).

"Fine," said the V.P. "Okay, Kenny, money always comes first. What do you expect by way of starting salary?"

Oh my! Despite all my thinking and talking, I still hadn't been able to settle on a number—in fact, had chickened out by hoping the other side would produce one first, thus giving me something around which to negotiate.

But I'd been jumped.

I took a deep breath, then, knowing I daren't further dodge the issue, mumbled something like, "Well, er....How about..." and named a number.

There was a long pause while the Times man lighted his pipe, which eventually was removed from his mouth and replaced by a soft smile and a gentle murmur:

"That sounds very reasonable."

Whereupon, of course, Sardi's—and life its ownself, to steal from Dan Jenkins—came crashing down around me.

"You idiot!" I silently screamed at myself. "You dolt!" "You clown!" "You fool!" "You nitwit!"

Very reasonable, indeed!

Hell, I told myself, I could have asked for *double* the damn number I'd stated, and, if not gotten quite that much, certainly a bunch more than the amount I'd proposed.

But there was no going back and the Times man's lil' ol' grin said he knew it. So he reached for my hand, shook it, and said, "Done deal, then," before moving on to other elements of the package.

That V.P. was a true gent. But it still enrages me to think of that meeting.

I edited *Golf Digest* from mid-1969 to early 1972, enjoyed most of the experience, but eventually became disenchanted with—given the ever more intensely "structured" nature of the enterprise under Times control—the increasing management component of my work compared to its creative element. Accordingly, over dinner at the Ryder Cup in St. Louis in the fall of 1971, I told Bill Davis, with a heavy heart, that I would be leaving as soon as he could arrange for a suitable replacement (our top feature-writer and my good pal Nick Seitz deservedly got and excelled at the job).

Disappointed as he was, Bill was kind enough to make me a contributing editor, which at that point was my only—and terrifyingly meager—income source.

But then came the opportunity of a lifetime.

I first briefly met Jack Nicklaus on his initial trip outside the U.S. for the 1959 Walker Cup at Scotland's Muirfield at the age of 19, but then from 1962, as editor of *Golf World*, had opportunities, primarily at tournaments he contested, to develop our acquaintance.

Increasingly impressed by his intelligence and exceptionally deep knowledge of playing technique—plus, of course, his already huge competitive achievements—this culminated in my hiring him in 1971 to contribute a monthly instructional feature to *Golf Digest* called "Lesson Tee." He and I agreed to create the material in what we called a "cartoon" format, whereafter I assisted him with the words while Jim McQueen, one of golf's finest instructional illustrators, provided the extensive full-color art. The series ran four years before becoming a top-selling book.

On turning pro late in 1961, Nicklaus had joined Arnold Palmer and Gary Player as a client of Mark McCormack's International Management Group, thus forming the famed "Big Three." But, by the middle of 1970, with the desire to control his own destiny increasingly irresistible, he parted amicably with McCormack and began assembling his own business team.

Jack's first hire, upon opening an unpretentious office near his North Palm Beach home, was a first-rate bookkeeper/office manager by the name of Esther Fink, who eventually won the record for long-term service to a wide variety of Golden Bear enterprises. Next aboard, initially in a part-time role as what he liked to call "head honcho," came an entrepreneurially minded and characterful high-school acquaintance of Jack's called Putnam Sandals Pierman, the scion of an Ohio based heavy-construction company. In turn, Put engaged a banker friend of his from Fort Wayne named Tom Peterson as full-time chief operating officer, along with David Sherman, a Columbus–born-and-bred lawyer, to provide legal services. Peterson then brought aboard, for general financial counsel and tax advice, Jerry Halperin, a CPA, lawyer, and senior partner with Coopers & Lybrand in that company's Detroit office. Jack himself hired Texan Bill Sansing, a marketing and advertising executive whose talents he'd gotten to admire through their joint long association with the Chicago clothier, Hart Shaffner & Marx, for overall business development and servicing.

I was the last to join what everyone invariably referred to as "the Group," largely, of course, due to my by then lengthy and close association with Jack, but also partially to the happy relationship I would long enjoy with Tom Peterson after we discovered at the 1971 World Cup in Palm Beach Gardens—won by Nicklaus with Lee Trevino—that we were exactly the same age, almost to the hour.

Very much part-time at first, my initial and ultimately long-term primary role was the development, creation, and rights sales worldwide of Nicklaus-authored literary products, primarily of an instructional nature.

As anyone engaged to work with any kind of superstar better quickly learn, that person's primary challenge is always time—meaning its shortage relative to the multiplicity of activities which they choose or are commercially persuaded to pursue.

Thankfully, in my case, our prior association had ground that factor home, along with Jack's perfectionism—his relentless determination that anything and everything bearing his name or likeness command, first, his total developmental input and, finally, his unreserved approval. Or, in short, working with the Golden Bear was about as far as one could get from the type of association—all too common these days, unfortunately—in which a superstar athlete approves a concept on the fly, relies on the collaborator to produce whatever has been agreed to, glances casually at the end product, then signs off on it with a don't-bother-me wave of the hand.

Oh, my, no!

The two questions I've been asked most about Jack Nicklaus over the years are, "What's he really like?" and "How did you work together?" Encapsulated, the answer to the first is—simply, but saying all that needs to be said—"A good guy."

Here's the answer to the second.

I would prepare, very carefully and thoroughly, questions and other forms of prompts via which to tape-record, in maximum detail, Jack's thoughts on whatever subject(s) we were to write about. Thus armed, I'd link up with him wherever and whenever he could find time and inspiration for such work, which, over the years, involved a wide range of locales.

One of the most pleasant for me was accompanying Jack on his annual two- or three-day practice trips to Augusta National the week before the Masters, where I'd generally watch him working on his game and updating his course knowledge in the daytime, then talk and tape-record with him well into the evenings. More common but less fun, because of the engine noise on the tapes—oh, how many stenographers over the years those huge Gulfstream power plants drove crazy!—was taping while he private-jetted around America and the world for tournaments, or on course design or other business projects. Our many sessions at his home were always enjoyable, if not always totally productive, given his unfailing attention to the activities and well-being of his large and, at times, exhaustingly energetic five children and their many friends!

Whatever, with the tapes transcribed, I would next create from them a first draft of what we both understood was no more than that. That material would then go to Jack for studied review in his own time, followed by revamping by me and further reviewing by him until he was satisfied that his requirements had been 100 percent met in every aspect of both substance and style.

Of course, this level of time-consumption and intensity of effort did ease some as Jack came to accept—as our relationship developed, with, by then, at least 2 million of his words recorded—that we had reached a stage of getting the stuff very close to where he wanted it the first time around. But, throughout the entire relationship, nothing ever went to press, from a single paragraph to a full-scale book, without his thorough input and approval.

Clearly, therefore, the primary key to succeeding and surviving in my role was devising some system whereby producing the maximum amount of material consumed the minimum amount of Jack Nicklaus's time.

Fortunately, the solution occurred to me quickly, beginning with the realization that gathering information on a one-shot basis—such as taping for lengthy periods for a single article, or even a single book—was definitely out. Instead, whatever time I could obtain with the Bear needed to be employed to gather material that could be utilized in a variety of marketable forms over an extended time period.

And, thankfully, that system worked.

For instance, over a near-40-year span, but with what I now regard as amazingly little of it together, we produced the following:

- 12 books, including Jack's second autobiography, *My Story*, and what its publishers' tallies indicate is the best-selling golf instructional volume of all time, *Golf My Way*, with nearly 2.5 million copies purchased in 11 languages since 1973
- many hundreds of articles for a variety of publications, headed by *Sports Illustrated*, *Golf Digest*, and *Golf Magazine*
- the longest-running worldwide-distributed sports newspaper strip in history, called "Play Better Golf"
- a wide variety of calendars, desk and pocket diaries, and date-pads
- a pair of two-hour-plus home-instruction/entertainment videos, also marketed under the *Golf My Way* imprimatur and covering all aspects of both the shot-making and strategical elements of excelling at the game
- the conceptual and scripting elements of a dozen or so network television specials

Obviously, all of these products were highly market-oriented in concept (and, hopefully, execution)—the output of one small division of Jack Nicklaus's ever-more-multifaceted business endeavors. But, in the sense that the primary thrust of the great majority of them was to promote better play, and thus the average golfer's greater enjoyment of (to borrow Jack's lifetime description), "the greatest game of all," my pride in both the quantity and quality of what we achieved has never wavered.

And I am proud to believe Jack shares that sentiment.

I write at such length about my engagement in the foregoing activities because they are what produced so many of the golf associations, experiences, and perspectives that have given life to this book.

However, all of my creative work with Jack was based on a financial sharing arrangement (and a most generous one proposed by him) rather than full-time employment, which left me free, as time and energy permitted, for other enterprises. Among those was serving, from its conception through the 32nd playing in 2006, as chief "words man" for Jack's much-feted Memorial Tournament, including the editorship from 1988 through 2006 of its award-winning magazine and the executive production and scripting of its highlights films/videos.

Somehow or other, I also managed to find sufficient time and pep for a couple of other enterprises. The most golf-oriented of the two was joint ownership, with the aforementioned David Sherman, of a television packaging company that coproduced, primarily with the BBC, more than 200 TV "specials." The bulk of these were high-profile pro-celebrity golf formats staged in summertime, primarily at premier British resorts, such as Gleneagles and Turnberry, then broadcast as winter series to pleasingly large prime-time audiences. With every top professional of that era participating, excepting Jack—we agreed this form of golf was not his cup of tea—plus just about every star American and British entertainer and athlete of the times who could break 50 for nine holes (and a few who couldn't!), the work provided me with experiences, some of which just had to be included herein.

As a lifelong book lover and gluttonous reader, my other primary non-magazine, non–Nicklaus-related activity was about a decade's worth of acquiring and editing books—including a few golf-related volumes—for a New York City–based publisher called Atheneum (long since absorbed into a larger house).

Regrettably, that essentially desk-bound, pencil-pushing labor failed to produce items for this volume, but I do want to salute the three people who made it first possible and then so highly enjoyable: Atheneum's founder and chieftain, Pat Knopf, a doyen of the American book business; what I always called Pat's head "do-it" guy, the company's chief operating officer, Marvin Brown; and my partner in the venture, one-time *Golf Digest* managing editor, writer *extraordinaire*, and fine friend, Larry Sheehan.

No one got filthy rich from that venture, but we had a ton of laughs.

I wrote this possibly overlong introduction to *Teeing Off* for what hopefully is an obvious reason: without awareness of an author's long and varied involvement with his subject, readers might rightly question his credentials for creating such a volume.

As more and more time has passed, I have regarded being able to make a living by working largely within a beloved field as one of my greatest blessings—surpassed only by the gorgeous blonde!

My gratitude to the game of golf, and to all those who encouraged and educated and befriended me along the way, is boundless.

I hope you enjoy what follows.

Ken Bowden, 2008

part one

PLAYERS

one

MY GREATEST
OF THE GREATS

Primarily, I suppose, because golf has been played so long (certifiably at least 600 years in one form or another), pretty much everyone earning a stipend by scribbling about it eventually becomes a golf historian to a greater or lesser degree. And, the deeper they get into that element of the gig, the more strong-minded I have found the majority become about who have been the greatest of the great players.

Being no different from my colleagues in that regard, it seemed appropriate to open this wide-ranging miscellany of a book—from what some of my family regards as a seriously misspent life!—with my own personal best-of-the best list.

Of course, the better my colleagues know the lore, the more certain I am that they will disagree. Which, to save even more late-night bar squabbling down the road, is why my 13 are presented in alphabetical rather than any attempt at a ranking order. ("You chicken!" I can hear already.)

WALTER HAGEN (AMERICAN, 1892–1969)

The most slashing swinger and dashing personality of the greats, "the Haig" rose from caddying to win two U.S. and four British Opens, plus a longtime-record five PGA Championships (eventually tied by Jack Nicklaus), four of them consecutively. Those and his many other victories were driven by a combination of swashbuckling, nerve, remarkable recovery skills (with the putter especially), and an almost infallible ability to intimidate his opponents. For instance, the dean of golf writers during his time, Bernard Darwin, wrote of him: "His demeanor towards his opponents, although entirely correct, had yet a certain suppressed truculence;

he exhibited so supreme a confidence that they could not get it out of their minds and could not live against it." Also known as "Sir Walter" for his ever-elegant appearance, best-of-everything lifestyle, and highly placed pals—he knew the Duke of Windsor well enough to call him "Eddie"—Hagen contributed more than any other champion to raising the image, social status, and living standards of golf professionals, both across and beyond America, the latter through several world exhibition tours. This he achieved by never treating himself nor allowing others to treat him in anything less than a first-class fashion. A quicksilver talker, perhaps his two most famous lines were, "I don't want to be a millionaire, just want to live like one;" and "Don't forget to smell the flowers along the way."

BEN HOGAN (American, 1912–1997)

"The Hawk" received more help with his technique early on than is generally known, mostly from fellow tour pro and lifelong friend Henry Picard. But for the greater part of his career—in huge contrast to today's stars with their personal instructors—Hogan famously "dug it out of the dirt," to use his classic expression for developing his game, alone and unaided. In which regard he was the most intensive experimenter/practicer of the great champions, ending with a quick, handsy, flat, laid-off, anti-hook swing that produced perhaps the most consistently fine shot-making in history. Hogan, throughout his peak competitive years, stoically fought the painful and debilitating aftereffects of a 1940 car/bus crash that almost killed him while driving home to Texas from California with his wife, Valerie, whom he saved from injury by throwing himself across her body a couple of seconds before impact. The greatest achievement of his late-developing career was winning the Masters, U.S. Open, and British Open in 1953—three of his nine major championship victories. The few people who achieved closeness to him had little doubt that his deeply introverted and relentlessly steely persona derived from parental psychological characteristics plus childhood trauma, and particularly his father's suicide within the family home when Ben was nine.

ROBERT "BOB/BOBBY" TYRE JONES JR. (American, 1902–1971)

Beyond dispute, golf's all-time greatest amateur. Bob, as he preferred to be called, won 13 of the game's premier championships of his era over a seven-year period, comprised of four U.S. Opens (1923, 1926, 1929, 1930), five U.S. Amateurs (1924, 1925, 1927, 1928, 1930), three British Opens (1926, 1927, 1930), and one British Amateur (1930)—the 1930 victories comprising a still unmatched single-calendar-year "Grand Slam." Immediately thereafter, with "nothing left to prove," and stressed to his physical and mental limits by the pressures of top tournament play, he retired at age 28 to study and then practice law in his hometown of Atlanta, Georgia. As a youth, Jones exhibited and was criticized for fits of anger when failing to meet his perfectionistic goals, but had disciplined himself to externally hide his naturally fiery temper by the time he attained his peak. In maturity, his good looks, modesty, courtliness, intelligence, articulacy, and literacy contributed to his becoming a national idol by the time he cofounded Augusta National Golf Club with friend Clifford Roberts during the Great Depression, followed by the creation of what became the Masters in 1934. Sadly, in his early fifties Jones began to suffer from a muscular illness known as syringomyelia that eventually left him horrifically crippled and in constant pain, yet he retained his sharp intellect and interpersonal gracefulness almost until his death in 1971.

BYRON NELSON (AMERICAN, 1912–2006)

Remarked the minister at "Lord Byron's" funeral, attended by almost 2,500 friends and admirers: "We can debate over which man was the greatest golfer, but there is no debate over which golfer was the greatest man." Nelson, who died at age 94, was indisputably golf's all-time consistently straightest hitter of a golf ball with every club, but the above epiphany drew from his personal qualities, most notably degrees of modesty, amiability, empathy, and devoutness extremely rare if not unique among professional athletes. As a player, the lanky Texan is credited with being the originator of the key elements of the modern golf swing, meaning more leg/body than hand/wrist-oriented. Despite his immense talent, Nelson competed intensively for the shortest time of all the greats (1932–1946), quitting full-time tournament play in order to fulfill his longtime dream of becoming a Texas rancher. Although the owner of two Masters and a pair of PGA Championship titles, plus a U.S. Open, he will best be remembered for the one golf record that many believe will never be beaten—11 straight tour victories out of his total of 18 wins in 1945 (and won by an average of 6.67 strokes).

JACK NICKLAUS (AMERICAN, 1940–)

With 18 major championship victories—20 if you count his two U.S. Amateurs—73 American PGA Tour wins, eight Champions (formerly Senior) Tour major titles, 113 professional victories worldwide, and receipt of just about every important award and honor golf offers, the "Golden Bear," as I write, remains almost universally acclaimed as the greatest golfer of all time. His professional major victories comprise a record six Masters, a record-tying four U.S. Opens, three British Opens, and a record-tying five PGA Championships over a 25-year span (1962–1986). In his early pro years Nicklaus's bulkiness, sartorial stylelessness, intensity of concentration and focus, and seemingly at times cold-blooded dethroning of everyone's then–golf hero, Arnold Palmer, cost him fan appreciation, despite his ever more dominating play. The path to his present immense level of popularity and respect was jump-started by early 1970s weight loss and other appearance changes, plus an ever warmer appreciation of and response to fans and the media. His renowned devotion to his large family, always his top priority, plus age-exacerbated physical challenges, led to his retirement from regular tournament play at the 2006 British Open at his beloved St. Andrews, where holing a lengthy birdie putt on the 18th green crowned a highly emotional farewell. But ever-increasing course-design activities—as of this writing he had more than 300 courses in play worldwide, with another 100-plus under construction or contract—ensure his continuing prominence and popularity in the game.

ARNOLD PALMER (AMERICAN, 1929–)

Inarguably, the most popular golf champion of all time, as connoted by his sobriquet, "The King," and the number, ardor, and loyalty of his fans—"Arnie's Army"—even as his playing powers waned with age. Other contributors to what at times appeared almost to be a form of love for the man were his ever-discernable enormous passion for and commitment to the game, his on-course facial expressiveness and uninhibited body language, his off-course friendliness and openness, and his peerless contribution to golf's greatest worldwide boom as it's premier player in the late 1950s and early 1960s, both in the flesh and through the relatively new medium of television. Inspired, taught, and relentlessly disciplined and motivated by a tough ex-steelworker-turned-club-pro father known as Deke, the powerfully built Palmer's style of play at its peak featured muscling shots and attacking holes with a degree of fearlessness and brio unmatched by either his predecessors or successors. Much trouble resulted, but the excitement of his often seemingly magical ability to surmount it—especially via super-bold putting—underlaid much of his appeal. Topping Palmer's long list of achievements were four Masters wins, a legendary U.S. Open title, and his 1961 and 1962 triumphs in the event that his participation almost single-handedly rejuvenated: the British Open.

GARY PLAYER (SOUTH AFRICAN, 1935–)
The third member of the famed "Big Three," with Palmer and Nicklaus, the, by comparison, diminutive South African was the first great golfer to train for the game like an Olympic athlete. Combined with immense ambition and unshakable resolution, his superb physical conditioning contributed to nine majors victories, comprised of three Masters, a U.S. Open, three British Opens, and two PGA Championships, making him one of only five golfers—and the only non-American— to capture all four of the world's premier golf titles. Among his other records is most tournaments played in most countries, for which he claims to have traveled more miles than any athlete in history—some 15 million and counting. Following six victories in Senior Tour majors when the fifties-and-up circuit went by that name, "Laddie," as many of his peers like to call him, remained competitive in his seventies on the Champions Tour. The father of six and designer of 200-plus courses worldwide, Player, when at home in South Africa, is a successful farmer and a champion horse-breeder, in addition to heading a foundation and operating a school serving needy children.

GENE SARAZEN (AMERICAN, 1902–1999)
His father, a deeply religious Italian carpenter, was highly averse to his son becoming a golf professional, but "Eugenio Saraceni" did so after contracting pleurisy and being urged to quit apprenticeship with his dad for less strenuous work (he changed his birth name because he thought it sounded too much like a concert violinist). Short but muscular, scrappy, opinionated, and ever positive in outlook, with an unorthodox grip, a self-taught, sturdy,

no-frills swing, and for most of his career an impatient "attack-everything" attitude, Sarazen was the first player to win all four of golf's "majors"—the U.S. Open (1922, 1932), the PGA Championship (1922, 1923, 1933), the British Open (1932), and the Masters (1935)—the others being Hogan, Nicklaus, Player, and Tiger Woods. Sarazen's most famed single achievement was winning his Masters in a playoff following execution of "the shot heard around the world," a holed-out 4 wood in the final round for a double-eagle deuce at the par-5 15th hole. Sarazen farmed on the side in his later years but relished the longest career of all the greats, extending from the 1920 U.S. Open at age 18 to the 1973 British Open at Royal Troon, where, age 71, he aced the infamous "Postage Stamp" 8th hole with a crisp 5-iron shot.

SAM SNEAD (AMERICAN, 1912–2002)

Golf's all-time greatest "natural"—i.e., instinctively fluent, rhythmic, and effortless-seeming—swinger of the club, greatly aided by an exceptionally fine physique, featuring a remarkable degree of double-jointedness. He possessed an uncomplicated approach to technique, as exemplified by his comment that what he sought most to swing well was to feel "oily." "The Slammer," as he was nicknamed for his immense power, was born, raised, and proud to play as the Virginia "country boy"—he took great pride in beginning the game by knocking around objects with clubs made from tree limbs rather than through formal lessons. However, he was known to be vastly shrewder, or "street smart," than he generally let on—especially with a buck or more at stake. Snead was amiable if never overflowingly friendly with people he liked because he'd found them trustworthy, but generally tight as a clam with those he didn't. His one career gap was the U.S. Open; he came close more than once, but his game infamously collapsed each time. It was suggested by a female fan—and Snead was a great lifelong fan of the ladies—that he tied with Tommy Bolt as possessor of golf's sexiest walk, or swagger, or strut. He was rarely seen in public—outdoors or in—without one of his "signature" straw hats, due to early and finally complete balding.

LEE TREVINO (AMERICAN, 1939–)

"Supermex's" immense popularity at his peak derived as much from possessing the most effervescent, crowd-interactive, on-course personality of the great champions as from his rags-to-riches background and superlative competitive record. Despite a seemingly unathletic physique and an entirely self-taught, highly unorthodox swing, Trevino was regarded by Jack Nicklaus as not only his toughest career opponent, but on a par with Ben Hogan as the finest shot-makers in golf history. However, of Mexican heritage and brought up in poverty in a Dallas maintenance shack, Trevino's rugged early life forged an off-course persona the polar opposite of his relentlessly wisecracking, bubbly public demeanor—as private, serious, and reserved as perhaps only that of his ball-striking peer, Hogan. After finishing fifth in the 1967 U.S. Open at Baltusrol as a total unknown, Trevino over the next four years won two U.S. Opens from Nicklaus, including the 1971 championship in a playoff, following which he added in the next two weeks the first of his two British Open victories, plus the Canadian Open. In the prior six weeks he had won twice, placed second once, and third three times. Trevino also won two PGA Championships 10 years apart (1974, 1984). The highlight of his highly successful over-50 career was defeating Nicklaus in the 1990 Senior Open.

HARRY VARDON (BRITISH, 1870–1937)
Although not known as such in his era—the term was a far-in-the future phenomena—Vardon was the first of what today would be called a "superstar," and he will be forever renowned for popularizing the game's most-used grip, "the overlap" (although it was first employed by a Scottish amateur named John Laidlay). Vardon used that grip, plus the then nearest thing to a technically "modern" swing, to win a still-record six British Opens (1896, 1898, 1899, 1903, 1911, 1914) plus the 1900 U.S. Open, among hundreds of other tournaments and "challenge" matches throughout his native U.K. He also broke innumerable course records in his three lengthy tours of the U.S., rarely losing an exhibition match even against the better ball of multiple opponents, and twice finished U.S. Open runner-up. During his 1913 U.S. sojourn, his and a contemporary English star Ted Ray's Open playoff defeat by a 19-year-old local amateur ex-caddie, Francis Ouimet, in the U.S. Open at Brookline's The Country Club near Boston marked the end of Britain's golf domination. That event also is regarded by many historians as the game's single most

popularizing occurrence in America until the heydays of Arnold Palmer. In 1903, shortly after repeatedly almost passing out during winning his fifth British Open, Vardon entered a sanatorium for lengthy treatment of severe tuberculosis. He eventually recovered sufficiently to capture his sixth Open eight years later, but, still a heavy pipe-smoker despite that trauma, died of cancer at age 67.

TOM WATSON (AMERICAN, 1949–)

After a shaky start on the tour at the relatively advanced age of 25—he was said to have "given away" the 1974 U.S. Open at Winged Foot with a disastrous final round, along with other tournaments—Kansan Tom Watson won 33 times on the PGA Tour, including two Masters (1977, 1981) and one U. S. Open (1982), plus a modern record–tying—with Australian Peter Thomson—five British Opens (1975, 1977, 1980, 1982, 1983). Jack Nicklaus was dramatically second or tied second in both of those Masters, as also in the 1982 U.S. Open, when Watson improbably but dramatically chipped in from heavy rough for a critical birdie at the par-3 71st hole— and also in two of the Kansan's five British triumphs—making Watson first with Arnold Palmer then Lee Trevino one of Nicklaus's three toughest career adversaries. On the Champions (formerly Senior) Tour, where Watson was still a factor at the time of writing, his majors wins included the PGA Senior Championship (2001), three Senior British Opens (2003, 2005, 2007), the JEN-WEN Tradition, plus two runner-ups in the U.S. Senior Open (2002, 2003). In 1971 Tom Watson graduated from Stanford University with a degree in psychology.

TIGER WOODS (AMERICAN, 1975–)

Some would argue that Eldrick T. Woods should already be acclaimed the greatest golfer of all time, based on his record at the close of 2007, at age 32, of three consecutive U.S. Junior Championship wins; three consecutive U.S. Amateur titles; 13 professional major championship victories comprised of four Masters, two U.S. Opens, three British Opens, and four PGA Championships; his "Tiger Slam" of consecutive U.S. Open, British Open, and PGA Championship triumphs in 2000, topped off by his 2001 Masters victory; scores of other amateur triumphs as a youngster, since followed by 80-plus pro victories around the world and almost $100 million in money winnings after turning pro in 1996. Others would claim that Woods still has to best Jack Nicklaus's record of 18 major professional championship victories to merit that designation. Whichever side of that debate a person happens to be on, pretty much everyone in golf agrees—given that Woods retains his, at the time of writing, excellent health, immense ambition, apparent dispassion about near billionairedom, and tolerance of the impositions and inconveniences of raging superstardom—he will eventually own the record that he claims has been his lifetime goal and principal golfing inspiration. And, again as of this writing, the "Cablinasian," as he calls himself (for his Caucasian/American Indian/African American/Asian heritage) showed zero signs of losing those qualities. Interestingly, the man who has inspired him the most as he aspires to demote him—Nicklaus, of course—believes that Woods's intelligence and recovery skills, with emphasis on superlative putting, are more critical weapons than his immense power with the long clubs. Woods and his Swedish former model wife, Elin, celebrated the birth of their first child, a daughter, in the summer of 2007.

Note: As I wrote at the outset, this is a personal choice. Other players who certainly merited consideration for inclusion include (again in alphabetical order): Tommy Armour, Severiano Ballesteros, Bill Casper, Sir Henry Cotton, Nick Faldo, Hale Irwin, Bobby Locke, Greg Norman, Dr. Cary Middlecoff, Johnny Miller, Phil Mickelson (unquestionably the best-ever lefty), Peter Thomson—and, going way back—Allan Robertson, the Tom Morrises father and son, James Braid and J.H. Taylor (the latter two, with Harry Vardon, making up the first "Great Triumvirate"), and even, maybe a couple of amateurs some readers might never have heard of, namely John Ball and Harold Hilton.

Anyway, let the debating commence!

two

INTERVIEWING THE "WEE ICE MON"

You've surely met at least one person in your life whom you will always remember vividly, sharp, and clear, as though it were yesterday.

For me, Ben Hogan possessed that sort of memorability.

I first met "Mr. Hogan"—it was only later that I summoned the nerve to call him Ben—in 1965 at Cuzzie Mingolla's Pleasant Valley course outside Worcester, Massachusetts, where he was playing in something called the Carling World Open. I'd become fascinated by the man's austere, enigmatic persona 12 years previously when he won the British Open at Carnoustie in his sole expedition to that championship. As the editor of *Golf World*, then a young but ambitious British monthly, I'd made an interview with the "Wee Ice Mon," as the Scots called him, the top priority of my annual U.S. visit.

The week prior to that Carling event, the late Dave Marr won his one major, the PGA Championship, at Laurel Valley in Ligonier, Pennsylvania—Arnold Palmer country—with Hogan, at age 55, placing 15th. There, I'd watched other pros watching Ben practice, standing well back as though he might bite if they got too close, all of them silent but clearly as awed as the fans by his succession of rifled 4 woods and seeming obliviousness to the gallery or anything but what he was doing.

The day after the championship, flying from Pittsburgh to Boston, I knew a number of top players were aboard the plane, but didn't realize Ben and his wife, Valerie, were among them until they emerged from the terminal building and looked around for a courtesy car to drive them the 50 or so miles to Worcester.

As he stood at the curb, squarely set flat white cap shading his deeply tanned face, the interminable cigarette jutting from the set jaw, a college-age kid loading bags into a courtesy car trunk stopped what he was doing, walked over to them, and gave them a big smile: "Mr. and Mrs. Hogan, welcome to Massachusetts. I have Mr. Sam Snead in my car ready to go to Pleasant Valley, but there's room for you as well. And I'm sure Mr. Snead wouldn't mind. Would you like to do that?"

Taking the cigarette from his mouth, Hogan stared at the youngster for at least 10 seconds before responding. What he eventually said was a curt: "Not particularly." Then, taking Valerie by the arm, he turned and walked toward another courtesy car that was pulling up nearby.

A posse of butterflies chased each other around my belly as I reassessed my chance of obtaining an interview with this wintry individual. When finally I breached the man's never-invade-my-space aura, as later that day he prepared in the locker room for a practice round, they began performing somersaults.

Dragging on another of his seemingly endless succession of cigarettes, Mr. Hogan stonily heard out my request, then paused for what felt like an hour while he considered it. Finally, he ground out, "See me in here after the round."

Thrilled but still jittery, I scampered back to my motel room and spent an intense couple of hours working on questions, finally coming up with a dozen that I prayed he wouldn't find too inane or intrusive.

The crowds for tournaments at Pleasant Valley in those days were immense. Even though they reputedly didn't get along, Hogan had played with Arnold Palmer, and it seemed like half the population of Massachusetts had accompanied them. Back at the course, I watched with growing dismay as the two superstars fought their way through a backslapping, pen-stabbing, autograph-besotted mob. Getting from the 18th green to the clubhouse door must have taken them half an hour. By then, I was pretty certain "Mr. Hogan" would be less than ecstatic to behold a fellow with a pencil and note pad at the ready when he arrived in the locker room.

At last he did so, gray-faced and sweaty, whereupon he walked directly to his locker, then sat in front of it without acknowledging me. Uninvited—indeed, still unacknowledged—I squatted hesitantly on the bench beside him. His only reaction was to lean over and slowly begin untying his shoelaces.

Did he know I was there? Did he remember he'd said to meet him after the round? Was it okay to speak to him?

Summoning sufficient courage to find my voice, I reidentified myself, thanked him for agreeing to talk to me, and asked the first question.

Silence. No body language to indicate he'd heard. Still totally focused on the shoelaces. What was probably a minute but felt like a week went by. Still no response.

Was he deaf? Couldn't understand my Aussie-Brit accent? I'd asked a stupid question?

Somehow I found the nerve to try again.

"Mr. Hogan, maybe I ought to rephrase—"

Before I could finish, around snapped the head, the icy blues locked onto mine, and the thin lips barely parted as the voiced rasped: *"Gimme time. Gimme time."*

And, of course, I gave Mr. Hogan all the time he wanted from then on to answer each question.

Which he did extremely carefully, only as fully as he deemed appropriate—meaning, three or four times, with either a blunt "Yes" or "No." But, all in all, after what had happened, surprisingly graciously once he realized they were not personally intrusive and had been compiled by someone who knew at least a smidgeon about golf.

He Wanted to Be Left Alone!

My next encounter with Bantam Ben was even more intimidating—in fact, one of the scariest experiences of my working life.

By then, utilizing my new American passport (*see page 172*), I'd moved to the U.S. after accepting *Golf Digest* chief Bill Davis's invitation to become editorial director of the magazine. Today, its offices in Wilton, Connecticut, are spatially splendiferous, but at that time were in a cruddy little box of a building—now a discount booze store—abutting I-95 and U.S. 1 in a tacky part of the town of Norwalk. Despite my fancy title, my space therein was all of 8 feet by 6 feet, or cell size—and with a leaky ceiling.

Ben Hogan at that time was still regarded by many golf fans as the world's greatest-ever champion, but, following his competitive retirement in 1968, had gradually become reclusive to the point of near invisibility.

Accordingly, pushed by my fascination with both the man and his record, pretty soon after I came aboard the magazine I began proposing we do a cover story/lead feature around the theme of "Ben Hogan Today." I figured that shining some light on "The Hawk" would do his legions of admirers a service, in addition to selling more copies of the magazine.

Everyone with an editorial voice at *Digest* liked the idea, except for the fact that they were certain Hogan would never personally cooperate, thereby making the piece undoable. After running into this roadblock a number of times in editorial planning meetings, I came up with an answer: we'd do the story by talking to people—family members if possible, friends, old rivals, business associates of his, etc.—who were familiar with his present activities and lifestyle, without even bothering to go to the man himself for the inevitable "No." Everyone eventually agreed, and I gave the assignment to Nick Seitz, then the magazine's top feature writer and later its editorial director.

As throughout my working life, at *Golf Digest* I preferred to answer my own phone, rather than go through the time-wasting process of having a secretary do so. I'll never forget the rainy, windy autumn morning it rang just as I was leaving for lunch. I reversed steps and picked it up.

"Is this Ken Bowden?"

"Yes."

"This is Ben Hogan. Listen carefully, because I'm only going to say this once. If you persist with this story I hear you are planning on doing about me, all advertising in your magazine and its associated publications by my company and its associated enterprises will be canceled immediately and for the foreseeable future. I hope I make myself clear. Good morning."

The dial tone buzzed in my ear before I could respond.

Uh oh! Pandemonium.

The Ben Hogan Company at that time, which Ben personally ran, was a major force in the golf industry, and thus an extremely important advertiser both dollar- and "image"-wise. *Golf Digest's* top management quickly caucused with the perpetrator of the crisis. Its decision was: the threatened action simply could not be allowed to happen.

Hence, "Get on the phone with Ben, Kenny, and talk him out of it."

Kenny tried, but Mr. Hogan would not take his calls.

"Get on a plane to Fort Worth, Bowden, and get in that damn Hogan plant and get to see the man, and *get it fixed*."

But if Ben Hogan wouldn't take my phone calls, what was the chance he'd see me, even if I showed up and prostrated myself on his doorstep? After the Pleasant Valley encounter, I figured the odds were perhaps a thousand to one against, maybe higher. Visions of a forced return to the freelance life—maybe even back to Britain—chewed at my mind. I slept very little that night.

Of *Golf Digest*'s three founders, Howard Gill knew Ben Hogan the best. A perpetually positive, cheerful, immensely likable man, and invariably the magazine's peacemaker and P.R. whiz, Howie finally got through to Hogan late the following morning. After about 20 minutes of closed-door phone conversation, Gill walked into my office, wiping his sweaty forehead but with a smile beneath it.

Mr. Hogan would meet Ken Bowden. The next day. In Fort Worth. At Shady Oaks Country Club. In the grill room. At noon.

Being a coward, I took Nick Seitz with me.

Ben Hogan's table at Shady Oaks at that time was located in the corner the farthest from the grill room entrance, backed on both sides by windows overlooking the course. Wearing a beautifully tailored dark gray suit, a blinding white shirt, and a deep maroon tie, he sat alone in the room and motionless, except for the movement of a cigarette to and from his lips. As the maître d' had conducted us into his presence, I stated my name and extended my hand. Staring into my eyes, he took the hand briefly, wordlessly, and without rising. Same with Nick.

A smiling waiter arrived as we seated ourselves.

"Drinks gentlemen? A cocktail, perhaps?"

"No cocktails," intoned Mr. Hogan. They were his first words in our presence. They were also his only words for what seemed like the next two hours.

Finally, the tension and embarrassment forced me to say something. Not as smoothly as I would have liked, I offered that, clearly, something was greatly disturbing him, that we were very sorry about that, that we would like to solve the problem if we could without hurting either of the parties, and that we very much wanted to hear whatever Mr. Hogan wished to say regarding the situation.

There was a long silence, but, once he began, Ben Hogan continued for longer than I'd ever thought I'd hear him speak without a break. He never raised his voice, there were no accusations, no invective (and, as I later learned, Hogan could be a world-class curser when provoked)—not even a repetition of the advertising-withdrawal threat. But the intensity of the delivery amplified the emotional depth of the message.

In précis, it was that Ben Hogan did not want people prying into his affairs. He had done his thing, and now he was retired and he wanted the world to forget about him. More than anything in life, he wanted *to be left alone.*

As he spoke, the magnitude of what was clearly a *need* as opposed to simply a desire for privacy became so clear to me, and had such a visceral impact on me, that I began to feel sorry for him; and certainly to wish that we had never undertaken "Ben Hogan Today." But the piece was far along, with all kinds of publishing arrangements cemented around it. There was also the factor that many people Hogan possibly cared about who had been interviewed might be disappointed, perhaps even hurt, if the remembrances they'd had of him and the compliments they'd paid him never saw light.

Once he'd finished speaking, after a suitable pause and as succinctly as I could under the pressure of the situation, I voiced both of those factors. And then, before he could respond, but after a quick internal prayer, I launched into the pitch that, in our strategy sessions, we hoped would not simply save the feature but greatly improve it.

To wit: whether he liked it or not, Ben Hogan, as one of golf's immortals, remained of consuming interest to a great many people around the world. Accordingly, much as he might desire otherwise, the only way to temper for a while, if perhaps never fully quench, the thirst for information about him was to provide some. And by far the best way to do that, obviously, was through the man himself, not only to ensure veracity but to exert control over the material *his* control. So—and here I mentally offered up another quick prayer—how about: instead of us fighting, we cooperate; perhaps, if he could see it that way, in the spirit of a public service by both sides.

That is to say, we would stop going around him in return for him— *this time and this time only*—as far as he saw fit, felt comfortable with, drawing back the blinds on the Ben Hogan of that time. By so doing, hopefully, he would give his legions of fans enough of what they wanted from him to sate their appetite sufficiently to *leave him alone* for a long time to come, hopefully (I assumed) forever.

I think it was that last factor that finally won him over. Whatever, after a long, contemplative silence, then more talk interspersed with further periods of reflection, Ben Hogan agreed to be interviewed, at length and in depth, for *Golf Digest* by Nick Seitz.

I never had before and never would again experience a greater sense of relief in a business situation.

three

HOGAN AT WORK

Ben Hogan's routine at that time, as I understood it had been since his competitive retirement and know it remained until deteriorating health forced cessation, rarely varied.

Impeccably clad in an expensive conservative suit and a subdued tie, he would arrive at his office soon after an early breakfast (invariably featuring his beloved scrambled eggs), work there until shortly before noon, drive in his treasured black Cadillac to the nearby Shady Oaks club, and eat his usual lunch at his usual table either alone or, if they happened to be around, with one or more of a small circle of friends. As the years passed, the food would increasingly be accompanied by alcohol—either vodka or white wine—but apparently generally in moderation.

From lunch, Hogan would go to his two lockers, change into equally immaculate golf clothes, take a cart and a bag of balls to one of two favorite spots on the course—but never the driving range—and hit shots, with either a caddie or an assistant pro doing the shagging. Frequently, he would also be accompanied by one or both of the club's mutts, whom, word had it, he loved more dearly than all but a handful of people (he paid for their burials on the premises). After that, he would clean up, drive home, and spend the balance of the day quietly with Valerie, invariably watching the evening news on TV before dinner.

Accordingly, with the "Ben Hogan Today" issue resolved and the lunch remains cleared, the great man announced to Nick and I that it was time for him to "go to work." His mood by then had improved sufficiently for me to dare a request. I told him we would regard it as a huge honor if he would allow us to watch.

As so often when he conversed while he thought through the implications, there was a lengthy pause, his steely blues finally locking on mine.

Then: "Can you keep *quiet?*"

I assured him that we could, and so a little while later we followed him out onto the pretty much deserted Shady Oaks course. There was no golf bag on his cart that day, but the apprentice pro he'd commandeered to shag balls brought along a handful of Ben Hogan Company 5 irons. As its founder, chief, and head designer switched from one to the next, hitting perhaps a dozen shots with each, then repeating the process, it became clear that this was a club-testing as well as a swing-workout session.

Now, this whole saga took place not long after what proved to be a highly controversial swing method called "square to square" had been heavily featured in and promoted by *Golf Digest* (despite the editorial director fighting Bill Davis so hard against running the stuff he almost got fired!). That afternoon, after what Ben obviously regarded as particularly good shots, he just couldn't stop himself turning to us with some comment like, "Square to square, huh? See how *square to damn square* I was there?" The look on his face as well as the tone of his voice told us all too clearly what he thought of our miraculous new system: garbage.

To Nick and I, sitting immobile in our cart but periodically whispering to each other in awe, almost every shot Hogan hit that afternoon seemed flawless, the ball boy rarely needing to move more than a step or two to retrieve the missiles (he told us later that Ben was actually trying to hit him, as apparently he always did his ball-pickers). After perhaps 90 minutes of this, Hogan waved the youngster in and walked over and sat silently in his cart next to ours.

Both of us thanked him for allowing us to watch, then, out of courtesy, I added that he seemed to be swinging and striking the ball as well as ever.

He was about to fire up a cigarette, but the lighter snapped shut as his head swung around.

"That shows how much you know about golf."

Stunned, I inquired, "Uh, ah, uh…What do you mean?"

"The height. *The height*, dammit. No damn consistency to the *height*. You couldn't see that, huh? Hell, you gotta have the *trajectory* right as well as the distance, you want to play this game. No wonder you guys'd ran all that square to square crap."

Ashamed of our ignorance and so pretty much speechless, we returned to the locker room, where, over a beer, Ben Hogan suddenly became as relaxed and amenable as I ever encountered him. And, this, indeed, to the point where, as we were preparing to leave after perhaps an hour of simply shooting the breeze, I felt comfortable enough to ask him what I regard as the $64,000 question: What would it take, financially, for him to reveal his famed but still much-debated "secret"?

The steely blues drilled right through me, but this time there wasn't even a second's delay with the words.

"A lot more than you guys could ever afford."

Although just about every tour and teaching pro on the planet, along with most of the golf writers who knew Hogan, had a theory, few public attempts were made during his lifetime to determine and reveal his supposed secret, probably for fear of lawsuits. Following his death, a seemingly endless parade of "authorities" have claimed to do so, in print and/or on videotape, frequently with widely differing conclusions.

So, with no one apparently ever coming up with the right price, the truth seems to be that the Wee Ice Mon took whatever he believed was the key to his phenomenal game with him to the grave.

And yet, when I asked him a few years later if he would swing the same way if he had to do it all over again, his reply consisted of the most stunning two words I ever heard him utter:

"Hell, no."

But, again, he would go no further.

Note: When Ben Hogan was honored at the 1999 Memorial Tournament, I had the good fortune to sit next to his widow, Valerie, during a dinner hosted by Barbara Nicklaus for her and a longtime friend of hers and Ben's. Mrs. Hogan was a charming if extremely self-contained woman who was surely the only person in her husband's life who truly understood him.

By then, I'd read over the years dozens of articles and book passages stating Hogan was born left-handed but had never thought to question him directly on the subject. So I asked Valerie.

"He was right-handed," she replied.

A few months later, having completed what she felt were her responsibilities regarding his remembrance, Valerie Hogan followed Ben to a place where hopefully he found a golf swing that was, at last, absolutely perfect.

four

THE NICKLAUS PSYCHE —
THE MAN

As mentioned earlier, the question I've been asked most about Jack Nicklaus over my many years of association with him is: "What's he really like?"

Trying to get past the vast amount already widely known about the man, here are my answers:

• As reflected by his lifestyle, plus the hundreds of friends he made both in and outside of golf, Jack's father, Charlie, was an extrovert, while his mother, Helen, was perceived by most people who came to know her well as introverted (the attraction of opposites?). My impression has always been that Jack inherited more of his mother's persona than his father's, but that the demands of being so public a figure for so long have produced ever more tempering of an inherited deep reserve. Certainly, no one close to him would regard him, in the popular sense of that word, as "outgoing." But that never seems to have stopped him from having "fun," especially with people he knows well and likes.

• Nicklaus's most defining personality characteristic to me has always been, to use a cliché, telling it like it is. His tactfulness and patience, especially with strangers or in formal social situations, have grown with maturity and experience. But in most circumstances—and especially with folk close to him—he always has had (and I imagine always will have) a tough time not unequivocally stating whatever he feels or believes, especially on subjects he knows well or feels strongly about. It is a trait that has occasionally caused him distress over the years, particularly via interpretations by certain elements of the media of what he regarded as honest and well-intentioned statements. His extreme verbal honesty, plus his certitude of

22

delivery, has also contributed to a reputation among certain tour peers for all-knowingness, as reflected by them nicknaming him "Carnac." However, you can be certain that whatever Jack says, whether right or wrong, comes straight from the heart, because there is not an ounce of deceit, dissembling, or duplicity in the man. In fact, I've never known anyone—and certainly no other "celebrity"—with less artifice or guile.

• To use one of my mother's expressions, it could be said that the greatest golfer of all time has lived since boyhood with a severe case of "ants in the pants." By that, I mean the hardest challenge Nicklaus routinely faces in life—with perhaps one exception discussed below—is inactivity. In all the years we've been associated, never once have I seen him simply sit still and stare into space, other than on an airplane, usually as a short prelude to taking a nap. Doing nothing to Jack is simply wasting time that could be used productively or enjoyably, or both, for golf, family activities, business, or recreation. Throughout his later competitive years, exercise routines filled what might otherwise have become flop-and-do-nothing-time. He regards driving or riding in cars for more than short periods as time wasted, which underpins his love of—and insistence upon whenever possible—helicopter and private-jet travel. Innate good manners enable him to "shoot the breeze" with friends during business gatherings and at social events, but such sessions are rarely long lasting. In short, blessed with an exceptionally high-energy metabolism, the Golden Bear is driven to fill every minute of every waking hour productively or enjoyably in one way or another. A wide variety of family pursuits have always ranked tops in that regard, followed, in his heyday, by golf practice and play, plus a multiplicity of business activities. His primary recreational pursuits are heavy energy burners, including multiple forms of hunting and "trophy-catch" fishing, along with tennis-filled fall and winter weekends, plus periodic skiing trips and summer boating expeditions. Hyperactivity personified, you ask? Well, one of his closest pals claims that even just thinking about who he calls the "Whirlwind" makes him want to go lie down!

• The primary mental factors underpinning Nicklaus's levels of achievement during his peak years are regarded by some authorities on the human psyche as aberrances, including especially egomania and self-absorption. Jack admits that—as with almost all super-successful people—he would never have gotten where he has without being power-fully ego-driven, but prides himself on almost always hiding that charac-teristic other than through his play. And, of course, that belief is power-fully supported by the great number of people—including peers, media, friends, fans, and employees—who regard him as the most gracious loser in his sport's history. As for self-absorption, or putting oneself first, although he and I have never discussed the matter, I doubt Jack would deny that at times it is a mandatory contributor to any form of immense success. And, sure, at one time or another, there is no doubt everyone closely involved with him has suffered to some degree from this trait (or necessity?), if only in losing a conflict between their desired plans and his. However, in this regard, along with many others, one of the most for-tuitous occurrences in his life was to marry a woman—Barbara Nicklaus, of course—possessed of the intelligence, love, grace, and skill to soften that trait whenever she's sensed it might be getting out of hand.

• Jack's greatest adversary, in my view, was never Arnold Palmer, Lee Trevino, Tom Watson, Augusta National, or the Old Course—or even the aches, pains, and other tribulations and limitations of attaining late mid-dle age (he turned 68 early in 2008). Plainly and simply, his greatest adversary has been food. Jack Nicklaus not only adores eating but can do it with such speed you think he must be cramming the stuff in his pock-ets or down his shirt front! Butter pecan ice cream seems to be his major weakness—and, when in a certain mood, the more the better. Indeed, for a man so incredibly disciplined in so many other elements of life, this trait's power made him overweight as a young man and now threatens him again as he ages. Thankfully, his voracious appetite does not include alcohol, beyond a very occasional beer or glass of wine (plain water is his regular tipple), and he stopped smoking cold turkey way back after years of a pack-a-day habit. Periodically throughout his peak playing years, he went on diets, making lunch-in-the-office, say, a dressing-free salad with a small dollop of water-canned tuna fish. But at other times? Well, every-one make way as the Bear heads for the table!

• Although clearly one of the most competitive beings in the history of mankind, Jack Nicklaus is remarkably non-adversarial in his dealings off the course. Sure, you'll quickly learn exactly where he stands on any given subject, and generally he will reciprocate by fully absorbing your "take," given only that he feels you are making sense. But my experience is that Jack dislikes dissension sufficiently to try to become a peacemaker in any situation that looks like it's getting seriously out of hand. Which, incidentally, an incident involving his son Gary leads me to believe has largely been the situation within the Nicklaus family unit. Examine the legend on the kind of drinking mug given as a peacemaking or plea gift to a parent by a misbehaving offspring, and invariably it will request, "Don't tell Dad!" In Gary's case, following some boo-boo, he presented the mug to Jack. The legend it bore was, "Don't tell Mom!"

• Some people love being alone, some can take it or leave it, and some definitely prefer company. With people he knows well, at least, Jack Nicklaus falls into the third group, an instance of which in my case occurred at a pre-Masters visit to Augusta. Jack had a top-floor suite at a downtown hotel, and me a regular room lower down. On the first night, the phone rang while we were preparing for dinner, and when I picked it up, an unmistakable voice said, "Hey, Kenny, this suite's got two bedrooms, so get out of there and come on up." Another example is the number of times friends as well as family members have stayed with the Nicklauses as house guests at major championships and other events all around the world.

five

THE NICKLAUS PSYCHE — THE GOLFER

The second-most frequent question I've been asked about Jack Nicklaus is: "What are the mental or temperamental factors that made him so great?"

Here's a stab at answering that, while hopefully avoiding the clichés that are so commonly applied to top athletes.

• Jack at his best was a superb shot-maker in every element of golf except, at times, wedging the ball short distances, but his primary competitive tool was always his brain. He would never claim to be super-smart in the academic sense, although, as his in-the-field mastery of the highly variegated arts and sciences of golf-course design illustrates, his learning capacity when enjoyably stretching his mind is top-notch. However, to my mind, no one in the game's history learned earlier and more deeply first the criticality and then the techniques of "managing" both one's psyche and the ins and outs of golf courses. In fact, to me, these have always been Jack's greatest competitive strengths.

• What for want of a better word I'd call "balance" is another key Nicklaus quality. Certainly in my time no one in professional sport has disciplined himself into being a more gracious loser than the Bear, as well as an invariably gracefully low-keyed winner. In which regard, level-headed as Nicklaus naturally was (and remains), I believe it was his dad and greatest spuporter, Charlie, who had the biggest hand in developing those traits, along with numerous other factors that contributed to his son's success. For example, Jack's autobiography, *My Story*, contains this passage: "My father taught me the single hardest thing a professional athlete has to learn, which is how to lose gracefully. Dad convinced me very early in my involvement with sports that *I had to accept the bad with the good* [my ital-ics]; that, however much it hurts inside, you smile and keep a stiff upper lip; that you shake the hand of the man who's beaten you, and you tell him congratulations, and you mean it."

• Perhaps the first hurdle Jack overcame to help him achieve such men-tal "balance" was understanding and accepting that even the very finest golfers always lose more than they win—an example being Tiger Woods in 2006 with a stunning nine victories but also 11 defeats. Patience has been said to derive from acceptance of reality, and I regard Jack's patience in achiev-ing his goals certainly as one of his primary competitive strengths. More than any other player of his time, in my view, he recognized and accepted that mistakes at golf are not only inevitable, but that the more he allowed them to upset him mentally, the more he would make. "The angrier you get at this game," he told me more than once, "the harder it beats you over the head." And the only defense against that, of course, is the self-control deriv-ing from unshakable patience combined with immense resolution.

• Another product of Nicklaus's remarkably balanced outlook was recognition that, among the best of golf's best, almost everyone possesses comparable physical "game"—meaning ball-striking and shot-making capabilities. Accordingly, very early on Jack recognized that success or fail ure depended primarily on the mental and temperamental strengths and weaknesses outlined above, both in his long-term career goals and the moment-to-moment strategical and tactical challenges of achieving them.

• Certainly, he religiously honed his immense physical capabilities as a golfer with more practice in his peak years than the world at large will ever know. When competing, however, he possessed the intelligence and the willpower to second those skills to his mental evaluations and decisions regarding the ideal plays, often even under the most extreme competitive circumstances, such as contending over the final nine holes of a major. Which explains why—although being both the most powerful straight driver of his time and a superb long- and mid-iron player—he so frequently sacrificed distance from the tee to ensure he avoided trouble, to achieve a flatter lie, or to obtain an easier approach angle. Additionally, he also often played for the safest rather than the closest-to-the-hole areas of greens, and trusted his putter to do the rest—especially when he enjoyed a lead toward the end of a championship, when the pressure squeezes hardest.

• It was, of course, the ever-growing competitive dividends of those elements of "balance" that enabled Nicklaus to easily ignore or brush aside both media and fan criticism that sometimes he played too "conservatively"—especially in his battles against his first great adversary, the inevitably "going-for-broke" Arnold Palmer. I never heard Jack argue that point, other than to perhaps quietly comment that golf's big winners are mostly the players who make the fewest strategical or tactical—i.e., judgmental—errors, as opposed to physical or ball-striking miscues.

• Balance, or discipline, in his tournament scheduling, it seems to me, also heavily contributed to Nicklaus's phenomenal record. Not all that far into his pro years there came a point where, although it was rarely publicly discussed, he regarded most of his "regular" tournament play primarily as preparation for the events that mattered the most to him, namely the four major championships. Combined with his dedication to family—he'd promised wife Barbara when they married that he would never be gone more than two weeks at a time—this obviated, or at least tempered, the "exhaustion" and "boredom" impacts of excessive competition that have limited or in some instances even completely wrecked pro golf careers over the centuries.

• And, of course, balance—or perhaps in this case one should say the immense self-discipline emanating from it—was exceptionally evident in Jack's practice regimens, both at home and at tournament venues. Especially when close to desired form, he would hit shots or practice-putt only to the point of achieving whatever goals he had set for himself that day, in terms mostly of mechanics with the full swing and "feel" with the putter. Once he was satisfied—whether after a hundred swings or strokes or less than a dozen—away went the sticks and with them the Golden Bear, on to another of his seemingly endless variety of activities. And, of course, such never-practicing-for-the-sake-of-practicing protected him from both self-inflicted mental stress and physical exhaustion, along with even more injury than he finally experienced. Most of all, he was in his heyday the tour's supreme example of never "working oneself worse" (in his view, incidentally, one of the average golfer's major failings).

• Particularly with the majors, a pattern of intensive preparation derived from Jack's deep dedication to his primary goals. Some might argue that these regimens exceeded a "balanced" approach, but they seemed always to be executed within a scheduling framework that leveled out whatever stresses were involved, particularly on the physical side. For instance, I recall family or vacation time, such as a boating/fishing trip, providing plenty of relaxation—of both body and mind—immediately ahead of many pre–major championship labors.

• Topping that preparation was obtaining detailed up-to-date knowledge of the upcoming venue, in relation, first, to the state of his game and, second, to potential course and weather conditions. This was achieved by playing and studying most majors venues via special trips, generally lasting from two to three days, often with just his caddie along, and invariably with vastly more attention to swing/stroke-tuning and hole-by-hole strategy than to score. For instance, even though he'd played in the Masters since the age of 19, pre-tournament work at Augusta National was never missed during his peak years. For the British Open, he would sometimes cross the pond a week or more early, not only to acclimate to the time change and other differences, but to play the course under the widest possible variety of conditions, especially wind direction and strength and turf texture.

• Both in preparing for tournaments and playing them, Nicklaus never hit a shot without knowing its exact distance. He had learned the immense psychological as well as physical (i.e., club selection) value of determining precise yardages from friend Deane Beman in practice rounds ahead of winning his first U.S. Amateur Championship at Pebble Beach in 1959. (The ever-astute Beman had copied precisely stepping off distances and noting them down from the practice's originator, a fine amateur player called Gene Andrews.) A few years after Jack's arrival on the tour in 1962, virtually every member was doing the same, and today studying and mapping the "geometry" and "arithmetic" of tournament courses has become an art form wherever professional events are played. Would that have happened without the Nicklaus example? Probably, but one still wonders.

• Finally, there was the matter of desire. Jack Nicklaus was gifted with a body that enabled him to excel at the physical necessities of playing superb golf, a mind that could master its bottomless well of mental demands, and the resources and opportunities to exploit those gifts. But, beyond all that, it was something deep down in the man's soul that made him, as I write, the greatest golfer of all time. My name for that something is desire. When winning mattered to him most, Jack simply wanted it more than anyone else.

six

THE BEAR UP CLOSE
AND PERSONAL

I was fortunate over the years to play with a lot of golf's top pros, but most often with the greatest of them all, a gentleman by the name of Jack William Nicklaus. Most of the hundreds of things I learned from him about the game are in the dozen books on which we collaborated, but a couple more come to mind as I look back over those memorable rounds.

Number one is a piece of advice to anyone contemplating a career as a professional tournament player. In a nutshell, no matter how good you think you are or can become, don't make a decision until you have actually *played* with a superstar or someone close. The reason is that this is the only way to discover how incredibly accomplished in every regard are golf's very best. Observing from the sidelines may give you a strong sense of their abilities, but comprehending the scale of the whole requires getting up close and personal.

Second, if you want to be a great player, don't ever hit *even one single shot* sloppily or casually. In a near lifetime of studying the game's best, Jack is the only player I never saw do that. Whether in a short warm-up session before a casual round or finishing up the final holes of a major when out of contention, he appeared to give every shot his absolute best effort, both mentally and physically, all the way from the tee to a tap-in. In fact, seeing others "half-ass" shots—including even meaningless putts—could get his goat. "Either give it 100 percent effort or pick it up," I and other annoyed or frustrated companions were instructed upon slapping halfheartedly at a "doesn't-matter anymore" shorty. And the lesson was clear: bad habits lead to bad play.

The first time I thought I might beat Jack Nicklaus was at the Augusta National many years before ex-chairman Hootie Johnson's course lengthening and other toughening set its primary architect, Alister MacKenzie, spinning in his grave.

Playing at plus-6 from the tips to my 4-handicap from the members' tees, Jack was giving me 10 shots in total. Somehow, playing out of my mind, I arrived at 18 even with him. He'd been kidding around with the other pro in the group coming off 17, but suddenly got that famous all-business look as we reached the final tee. "Let's see," he said, "we're all square and you get a shot, right?"

Well, 10 minutes later, the denouement was me handing him 10 bucks. Playing the hole as though the Masters was on the line, he'd made birdie 3 against my bogey 5.

"Boy, I murmured," as we walked off the green, "are you one competitive son of a gun or what?" He grinned and patted me on the shoulder. "Hey, Kenny, 10 bucks is 10 bucks, right."

If you think that showed just how competitive the man was, try this one on for size.

Jack, his longtime friend Pandel Savic, and I occasionally made a threesome at the Loxahatchee Club he'd designed not far from his home, where Pandel and I had also become members.

One Saturday morning, Pandel decided, just for fun, to enter Jack in the club's routine men's-day event, but remembered to mention it only after we'd played three or four holes. Jack stopped in his tracks and said, "You mean, I'm playing in a tournament?" then, when Savic nodded, asked, "For money?" Pandel told him he might collect, oh, $50 or $60 if he happened to win low gross.

On we went, but, just like that, Jack's focus on his game intensified to a point where conversation, which had been three-way, light, and sprightly, dwindled to largely between Savic and myself. Walking off the 18th green, I added up our scores. J.W. Nicklaus had produced the best of them with an almost flawless 6-under-par 66.

Informed in the pro shop that he was now $70-plus wealthier, the grin on the great man's face would have made you think he'd won the Grand Slam.

In all our long association, I beat Jack Nicklaus once—and gross, no strokes, believe it or not—playing with him, his son Steve, and Lenny Davis, a pal of all of ours from California, in a practice round before Jack contested a Skins Game at Mauna Lani on Hawaii's Big Island.

The Bear had shot a par round of 72. By holing out from a bunker at the final green, I nipped him by a stroke, but awareness of that amazing achievement did not strike any of us until Lenny, totting up the numbers as we quenched our thirsts, exclaimed, "Hey, Jack! Kenny beat you, 71 to 72!"

A surprised expression on his face, Nicklaus demanded, "Gimme that card!" which he checked very carefully before agreeing, "By golly, so he did."

"Jack," I said, "this one you have just *got* to sign for me."

Pulling out a felt-tip, he asked, "What do you want me to write?"

"How about," I responded, "'Ken Bowden is a truly great golfer'?"

I got a flash of the steely blues, but he nodded as he began writing, and I thought he'd finished when he decided to add a postscript before signing his name.

Back came the card and there it was, just as I'd requested, neatly and boldly inscribed: "Ken Bowden is a truly great golfer."

But then, in letters twice the size of their predecessors, came the postscript:

"BULLSHIT!!!"

Regardless, elegantly framed, the card will continue to occupy a place of honor on my office wall until I go to my reward.

A NEEDLER NEEDLED

Jack Nicklaus has long been almost as good at "needling" as he was at golf—to a point, in fact, where many of his friends and associates regard how much he "sticks it" to people as the best measure of how much he likes them or otherwise.

Over the nearly 40 years I worked with him, I can recall only one instance of getting the better of him, meaning producing a retort that stopped him cold.

We were at Pebble Beach ahead of an AT&T Pro-Am preparing to tape one of a series of TV programs for ABC Sports, featuring wide-ranging conversations between Jack and his chief adversaries—Tom Watson, in this case.

Producer Terry Jastrow's plan was for Jack to tape the intro to the show before Tom arrived, meaning that I, as the "words" man, was required to draft a piece of script to go on the teleprompter as an aid to Jack in recording his opening. Accordingly, he and I talked for a minute or two about what he wished to say, which I tape-recorded on my hand-held machine as an aid to producing the required piece.

Like most professional athletes, Nicklaus always wanted his scripted material to sound "natural," in the sense that the words came across as closely as possible to the way they did when he talked extemporaneously. Unfortunately, however—as all writers faced with this type of challenge know only too well—ad lib spoken language by the great majority of people is invariably gobbledygook when committed to paper, compared to even the simplest written form.

We had plenty of time before Watson arrived, and, in light of an earlier incident in which Jack had not cared for my written version of his spoken thoughts, I decided to have a little fun with him.

First, I wrote a hopefully acceptable opening, but then persuaded the teleprompter operator to type Jack's exact words from our planning conversation into the machine ahead of that real script, so that his conversational language was what he'd encounter as he began rehearsing the opening.

And it worked beautifully.

The great man got about two sentences into the literal transcription before he threw up his hands and, turning to me, exclaimed, "Kenny, what is this garbage?" Then, appealing to Jastrow, "My lord, I can't say this stuff, Terry. Nobody talks like this, do they?"

Obviously in on the joke, Jastrow just shrugged his shoulders, whereupon I interjected quietly, "Jack, what you were reading is an exact transcription of what you said when we talked about the opening's content just a little while back."

For the only time in all the years I've known and worked with him, Jack William Nicklaus was—at least momentarily—totally speechless.

seven

"ONLY A GAME"

The good fortune of working at something beloved took me to over 100 major golf championships. Many still trigger rich memories, but the one that sticks in mind the most is the 1977 British Open at Turnberry.

It started with our living arrangements.

Accommodations at "The" Open are always a challenge for the hoi-polloi (which includes most of the media), but we'd heard about a small bungalow that was relatively close to the course and sounded cozy, so we rented it for the week.

Arriving there after a traffic-choked drive from the Glasgow airport, my bursting wife rushed to the bungalow's one bathroom as I began schlepping in luggage. As I hauled the first case, a loud crash erupted, followed by a cry for help.

Rushing to the bathroom, I discovered that the toilet's entire flushing mechanism—an old-time hefty metal lever and chain arrangement—had collapsed into the bowl, narrowly missing Jean's head. An hour later, the kitchen's wall-mounted can opener fell off, splattering our first dinner course—minestrone—far and wide. As we prepared, exhausted, for an early night, I eased the master bedroom's blind slats closed uneventfully, but then attempted to further stave off the early Scottish dawn by drawing the drapes. *Crash!* Down came rod, rings, drapery, blind, screws, and plaster, most of it on top of me.

From then on, we tested the remaining appurtenances extremely gingerly before attempting usage.

But the golf made up for what we christened "Crumple Cottage."

Turnberry's magnificent Ailsa course was hosting its first Open. Perhaps saluting that, the golf gods decreed four days of almost tropical weather, rendering the course virtually defenseless—certainly compared to its next Open nine years later when only Greg Norman, victorious at even par, mastered horrendous rain, wind, and savage rough.

Jack Nicklaus was still golf's dominating figure in 1977, but with Tom Watson beginning to rock his throne—as witness Watson's 2-shot triumph in their Masters *mano-a-mano* three months earlier. The first day at Turnberry both shot 68 against a par of 70 for the then 6,875-yard course, two more than leader John Schroeder, whose conclusion of his 4-under round long past their evening deadlines threw Britain's daily newspaper golf writers into a major tizzy.

Mark Hayes scorched a scorching course with a 63 on day two, tying the British Open single-round record with Johnny Miller's U.S. Open number, while the Bear and his heir apparent each matched par. Leading them by a stroke with 71–66 was the present NBC TV analyst, Roger Maltbie, who immediately became an honorary Scotsman when the local press discovered his mother was born near Glasgow. At that point, some 20 players were still contenders at 5 or fewer strokes back of Maltbie.

In round three, what many still believe to have been the greatest two-man duel in golf history began quickly and never let up. Paired together, playing off each other, and playing superbly, the 37-year-old Bear and the 27-year-old who would become his last great rival spread-eagled the field with matching 65s, both of which could have been a couple of strokes lower. At day's end, Ben Crenshaw, with a 66, remained the lone possible last-day challenger at 3 back.

The final round became a pure head-to-head knock-down-drag-out almost immediately, the rest of the field quickly forgotten. With five birdies between them, Jack and Tom were tied after eight holes. The previous day a storm had briefly sent them for shelter off the 9th fairway. This time they stopped on it to inform the overpowered "stewards" (marshals) that they would not continue play until the rampaging crowd was at least sufficiently controlled to give them clear sight of fairways and flagsticks. Somehow, the harried volunteers and handful of wool-uniformed, shirt-and-tied, sweat-soaked and puce-faced cops more or less complied.

After slipping marginally around the turn, Watson cut his deficit to 1 with a birdie at 13. On the 14th tee, as his eyes met Nicklaus's, he said, "This is what it's all about, isn't it?" "Darn right," was the response. They halved the tough par-4 when Watson missed from seven feet for birdie.

The par-3 15th deeply bruised the Bear. Tom missed the green left, 60 feet from the hole, while Jack knocked his tee shot within easy 2-putt range. Watson then rattled the pin with a speeding, bumping putt, the ball diving cleanly into the cup—a miracle shot. When Jack failed to match the deuce, they were tied again.

A half at the tricky 16th, two perfect drives at the par-5 17th, then a Watson long-iron to 15 feet after Nicklaus's second drifted short and right of the green. Tom narrowly missed his eagle attempt, but Jack's six-footer for a matching birdie after a good chip was still a must. He shaved the hole on the correct side with a minuscule misread. One back, one to go.

A perfect long-iron tee shot from Watson at 18, then a pushed-sliced 3 wood from Nicklaus, stopping in gnarly rough inches from an immense bank of gorse bushes. Away, Tom fizzed a 7 iron 18 inches short of the cup. Somehow, the Bear, the eternal battler, got his ball on the front of the green 30 feet from the pin—then holed the putt! Watson, now needing his "tap-in" for victory, holed it quickly to win with 65 to Nicklaus's 66—268 to 269 for the 72 holes. Third at 11 strokes back was Hubert Green.

Almost every reporter of the championship, television particularly, highlighted the truly warm manner in which Jack congratulated Tom. The loss hurt the Bear for sure, but the fact that he had been beaten by marginally better play, not defeated himself, salved the wound, as it did on numerous other occasions throughout his career.

Jean and I had made a dinner date with the Nicklauses for that evening, but, concerned about their feelings, I suggested to Jack after things began winding down that maybe we should cancel it; that he and Barbara might prefer to spend what was left of the evening quietly alone.

"What's the matter with you?" he responded. "Don't you want to eat?"

After I explained my feelings came the words I remember best from our long friendship and business association.

"Kenny, how about you run along and get cleaned up for dinner. Barbara and I will be just fine.

"After all, it's only a game."

eight

GOLF'S ULTIMATE PRO

Although periodically he'd have company and thus assistance on the road—his wife, an agent friend, or his beloved African American caddie Herman Mitchell—the most self-sufficient golf superstar I got to know was Lee Buck Trevino.

Here's my best-remembered example.

The frequently not-so-merry Mex—his private persona was normally as low-key and self-contained as his public one was extroverted and ebullient—played in six editions of a pro-celebrity golf series coproduced with the BBC from 1974 through 1993 by a company of which I was a joint principal.

With world-class entertainers and headliner athletes from other sports always participating, we needed to provide top-of-the-line limo and other ego-massaging travel and general "gofer" services for the weeks of shooting, not to mention the finest accommodations and other amenities available (Gleneagles and Turnberry hosted most of the series). And, with everything then so new for him, the first time I negotiated Lee's participation, he readily agreed to utilize those services.

However, I'll never forget his response when I called him ahead of his second series regarding traveling from his then-home in Dallas to the wilds of Scotland—with, of course, the news that we were again ready and eager to arrange his entire trip.

For a world-renowned professional athlete, his response was stunning. All he wanted to know was what time on what day we required him to be at the hotel for our first production meeting. After I told him—6:00 PM on a Monday, or whatever—the most I could get out of him on the matter, somewhat laconically, was, "Okay, got it. I'll be there."

In light of travel boo-boos we'd had over the years with some of our show-biz giants, that situation got my stomach churning. But, exactly at the appointed time on the appointed day, the door of our meeting room at Gleneagles opened, and in walked the star of the show, surprisingly fresh from having made the trip entirely under his own steam.

Of all the professionals who played for us—and they included every "great" of the period except Nicklaus (he and I had jointly agreed the format was not his bag)—"Lee Buck," as I invariably called him, also required the least prodding, shepherding, or hand-holding.

Arriving on the dot of the appointed time at each evening's production meeting, he'd order a light beer, then ask, "You get what you wanted from me today?"—to which the answer invariably was, "You bet!" Then he'd listen carefully to the production team's to-and-fro regarding the next day's shoots, and particularly the times of the camera calls, maybe ask a question or two, then stand up and say, "Okay, got it. So you're done with me, right?" Whereupon, short of some evening social appearance with sponsors to which he'd agreed (and, boy, well as he handled them, how he disliked those!) he'd go to his room, flop on the bed, order room service, watch TV, and fall asleep early.

Overall, Lee Buck participated in 50 of our nearly 150 pro-celebrity programs, invariably shot over nine holes at the rate of two per day. Throughout that marathon, he was always a minute or two early for camera calls, always wearing the required outfits, always warmed up and ready to play, and always full of new jokes, one-liners, technique tips for the celebs, and general make-everybody-happy chitchat and banter.

No other pro—including those with entourages—came close to matching his unfailing professionalism.

Which, of course, is why we hired him so often.

And also why, at his request, we happily handed him the check for his upcoming services the moment he arrived!

Why So Reclusive
Once the last putt was holed, Lee Trevino at his peak was surely the most reclusive of golf's superstars, very rarely partying publicly or even dining out unless obligated to for a business reason or at a close friend's or

associate's request. On the road, room service and TV seemed to be his almost invariable evening regimen.

I once asked him about that. The answer came quietly:

One night way back my wife and I at the time, we're at some tournament and we go out to dinner at a place she really liked. Just the two of us.

So, we've settled in and had a drink and, just as the waiter brings the entrees, this drunk old guy—really blasted—staggers over with a piece of paper in one hand and a pen in the other and yells, "Hey, Lee Trevino! How ya doin', man? Listen, you're my favorite and I just gotta get your damn autograph."

Our table was small and really crowded with stuff. So, when the waiter arrives he only just about finds room to put my wife's entree—some kind of pasta dish all juicy and steaming hot—down in front of her. And this drunken clown, he sticks out his arm and, in trying to push her plate aside so he can put the bit of paper down for me to sign, he shoves this bowl of red-hot food smack into her lap. And, of course, the stuff burns her badly through her clothes and, quick as we can, we have to get out of there and get her to the hospital.

And, although that was the worst, it was far from the first time something like that had happened, or some idiot I'd never seen in my life before who wanted to be my instant best buddy gave me grief.

And so after that night, I promised myself, "That's it. From now on, it's room service every time I can."

GOTCHA!

Sure, there was Arnie and Gary and Billy Casper, then Johnny Miller, and finally Tom Watson, but the record indicates that Lee Trevino was Jack Nicklaus's toughest opponent. What sometimes surprised me, in that light, was how easy-going and mutually admiring their relationship seemed to be, with Lee Buck forever insisting Jack was the all-time greatest, and Jack calling Lee as good a shot-maker as he ever competed against, on a par with Ben Hogan.

Eventually, however, the Bear realized that his friendly rival's incessant chatter during critical rounds—although I doubt he ever regarded it, as some others did, as deliberate gamesmanship—was not helping his concentration. Whereupon the next time they were partnered together in a tournament, with typical frankness, Jack told Lee on the first tee that he did not wish to talk a lot during the upcoming round.

Nicklaus still laughs as loud as everyone else when he reports Trevino's response:

"That's fine, Jack, because you don't have to talk, man. All you have to do is listen."

nine

THE GREATEST ROUND
EVER PLAYED?

The greatest round of golf of all the thousands I've witnessed in covering the game for some 50 years was the 63 produced by Johnny
Miller in winning the 1973 U.S. Open at Oakmont.

After a third-round 76, the rangy Californian with the mop of surfer-
blond hair would start that Sunday 6 shots behind a dozen other players,
including Jack Nicklaus, Arnold Palmer, Gary Player, and Lee Trevino.
Certain he was out of contention, that morning Johnny had asked his
wife, Linda, to pack and arrange transportation to the Pittsburgh airport
so they might catch the earliest possible ride home after he finished as he
foresaw himself—an also-ran.

Where things began to change was on the driving range, while he was
warming up, when Miller heard an internal voice tell him—and tell him
three times, no less—to open his stance. He remembers thinking, "I really
don't know if I want to try that," but eventually decided to give it a go.
And the rest, of course, is history. (A female gallery member, informing
him that she was a clairvoyant and assuring him that he was definitely
going to win, might also have contributed at least a smidgeon.)

Not to get too detailed, but the approach-shot aspects of the round are
stunning enough to be worth recalling.

Always renowned for exceptional iron play, Johnny got inside six feet
on five of Oakmont's wicked greens, including once with a 9 iron for a
tap-in birdie; inside 10 feet on two holes; and inside 15 feet on three. Sure,
he was helped by the fact that rain had softened arguably America's most
brutish course's infamously super fast putting surfaces (causing its
appalled leadership to asterisk that factor on his scorecard later displayed

in the clubhouse!). But Johnny missed not a single green in regulation in what can only be called a display of genius-level approach play, and also did not leave himself a single downhiller among his total of 29 putts.

Sixty-three has been shot 22 times in the four majors at the time of writing, but Miller's was both the first and the only such score to produce victory—by 1 shot over John Schlee.

Miller said, as he prepped for the 2007 Open at Oakmont as chief NBC TV analyst, that many players, including even Tiger Woods, asked him, "How the heck did you *do* that?" His answer: "Well, that clear voice said, 'Open it up,' and I did, and every hole I was right at the pin, dead underneath the cup, all 18 times, averaging about nine feet for birdie. Sounds like I'm bragging, but, the bottom line, it was a crazy round." Miller—who also won the British Open in 1976 by 6 strokes from Nicklaus and a 19-year-old then virtual unknown from Spain named Severiano Ballesteros—added, "And I wish I'd had Ben Hogan caddying for me, because I believe he would have said, 'You've got to be kidding me!'"

Proud as he is and always will be of the Oakmont achievement, it should be added that Miller believes that, although his may have been the best single round in golf's toughest major, it was not the best perform-ance overall in the U.S. Open. That, he says, belongs to Woods, with his 15-stroke victory at Pebble Beach in 2000, and particularly his putting. "Never lipped out one putt in 72 holes," Johnny recalls. "And, to my knowledge, never missed a putt inside eight feet on those bumpy old greens. Amazing!"

As the years passed and his own putting drove him ever crazier, Johnny Miller achieved another "greatest," that as being television's most popu-lar golf commentator, at least with the average American fan and student of the game. And, of course, the factor that got and keeps him there— unrelenting biting honesty, running sometimes to truly caustic observa-tions about tournament plays and their top-name perpetrators—also makes and keeps him the least popular with many of those he critiques. (Questioned on that subject, his overall reaction could be summarized as, "I don't give a hoot," awareness of which naturally further angers the pro game's more thin-skinned gladiators.)

Pretty much by chance, I discovered the four qualities that I believe contribute most heavily to Johnny Miller's long-standing kingship of golf on the "box" when, in 1977, he played in the aforementioned pro-celebrity TV golf series that a company I co-owned and coproduced with the BBC (*see page 156*).

In a nutshell, they are high intelligence; exceptional insight into the immense range of mental and physical factors that make even the finest golfers perform both brilliantly and badly; unusual articulacy for a long-time pro athlete; and, last but certainly not least, as deep an understanding of all aspects of both golf technique and its playing strategies and stresses as any top player or teacher I've encountered.

Where all of this became evident was one gorgeous day at Gleneagles in Scotland, when, having completed videotaping a match exceptionally early, I asked Johnny, off the cuff, if he would care to contribute a half-hour of programming to a series of instructional shows that we were also coproducing with the BBC, featuring the biggest "names" among the professionals participating in our pro-celeb contests.

He asked what type of material we were looking for, and I suggested that a half-hour exposition on the full swing "The Miller Way" would make a great addition to our series.

Johnny thought about the idea for a few moments before agreeing, whereupon I asked him how long he would need to prepare himself. We were standing on a tee on the back nine of the King's Course, and his response was to ask if that was a suitable location. When I told him it was, he responded, "Fine. Someone get me something to wipe my face, then I'll be ready as soon as you have the crew and cameras positioned."

And, boy, was he ever!

Fifteen minutes later, after we told him we were set, he took his position, the clapboard clacked, and off Mr. Miller went. And not only was he ready, we discovered, but amazingly prepared in terms of content, the ideal sequences of presenting it, and the best camera angles for full-figure action and other types of shots. Perhaps most surprising of all, he was also almost faultless in terms of literacy, verbal delivery, and tying words tightly to pictures. It was, indeed, as sleekly professional a performance as any of us on the production team had experienced, even from longtime superstars of the cinematic art form. And all shot in only a few minutes over the duration of the finished product, and in a manner and sequence that would make editing and embellishing the footage a stroll in the park.

As the director called the final "cut," the entire crew—as hard-boiled and cynical a group as most such teams about "amateurs trying to be actors"—abandoned its equipment, clustered around Johnny, and gave him a huge round of applause.

I recall that his 63 to win that Open got a louder and longer reaction, but surely no more heartfelt.

ten

GOLF'S FIRST GREAT
NON-BRIT OR YANKEE

There never has been and—I would bet heavily—never again will
there be a champion golfer with an appearance, a temperament, a
demeanor, or a game comparable to that of Bobby Locke.

Born of Irish parents who had emigrated to South Africa's Transvaal,
Arthur d'Arcy Locke, to give him his real name, although no one in golf
ever addressed him as such, was widely regarded as the first of the game's
great non-British or -American players.

Even in retrospect and precis, his achievements are stunning.

They included two South African Amateur titles before the age of 20,
nine South African Opens; the championships of Ireland, New Zealand,
Canada, France, Egypt, and Switzerland; four British Open victories plus
two runner-up finishes; third place in two U.S. Opens; and, perhaps most
remarkable of all, in 1947, at the age of 30, second in money winnings on
the American circuit on his first visit to the USA, with seven victories, two
runner-up finishes, and, following his first tournament—the Masters,
where he placed 15th—no finish worse than seventh. It should also be
noted that, during the Second World War, he had survived 1,200 hours as
a bomber pilot.

Following a youthful litheness, much of Locke's golf success was
achieved with a good 20 to 30 pounds of excess weight, a notable portion
of it residing in pronounced facial jowls; a temperament so placid and
slow-paced that it could take him 10 minutes on a locker-room bench to
change from street into golf shoes or back again; and a flat white cap
matched colorwise by wooly stockings snuggled into invariably dark and

ultra-baggy plus-fours, frequently topped by a white dress shirt into which was tucked a tightly knotted tie.

Gamewise, Locke possessed a long, deliberate swing involving, by today's standards, a stunning amount of roly-poly body work that heavily drew or flat-out hooked every shot he struck, from driver through pitching wedge. Additionally, contributing most heavily to his record was his phenomenal skill with an old rusty-bladed, hickory-shafted putter that he took way inside the line on the backswing before rapping the ball firmly on a meticulously pre-investigated line—often following it with an air of calm certainty before it got to the hole, at which point he would lightly tip the brim of his cap as the ball so frequently toppled in either dead center or from one side or the other.

Highly unlikely as it seemed visually to authorities on technique, most of his father-inspired but self-taught technique Locke claimed to have emanated from his reading of Bobby Jones's books and studying of Walter Hagen's slashing action.

Temperamentally, Bobby Locke had—and probably still has—no peer in golf. Examples include heroically shooting a (in those times) stunning score of 70 at St. Andrews after triple-bogeying a hole in the first round of his first British Open; turning in a 69 on the way to his initial victory in the championship after another triple; and, following yet another 3-over a year later, four birdies over the ensuing six holes to successfully defend the title. In other words, nothing—but *nothing*—ever seemed to upset him.

Perhaps the most appropriate footnote to his career is that he was never defeated over 72 holes in his homeland, where in 1946 he shockingly beat the legendary Sam Snead in 12 out of 16 challenge matches.

I got to know Bobby Locke initially through journalism, but our friendship deepened after I returned to America, where in his later years he would vacation in Vermont with his American-born wife. There, I discovered a socially down-to-earth but seemingly ever-congenial man with a wry sense of humor who enjoyed easygoing rounds at the Rutland club with just about anyone seeking a game—often followed by some joyful solo or group singing, accompanied by himself on a ukulele, and especially after inhaling a sizable quota of his beloved Pabst beers.

In his heyday, rather than attempt a called-for fade, I remembered Locke, in tournaments at the famed Sunningdale club near London, taking one or even two more clubs than his opponents, in order to play his standard heavy draw or light hook to the 10th green on the New Course over a stand of tall trees tightly lining the right side of that long par-3.

I knew many of the European tour players had kidded him about this highly unusual but supremely confident tactic, and so one day as we were waiting to play our approaches I decided to give him the business.

"Bobby," I told him, "I believe the reason you never played a fade, even at that hole at Sunningdale where it's absolutely the correct shot, is that you flat out *couldn't*. And here's my offer to find out the truth: you fade this approach to that green down there and I'll buy you a case of Pabst. But you draw or hook it in, then you have to give me a half-hour putting lesson — *for free*."

Locke threw me a long look, followed by a tight grin.

"Maarstah," he said — he used that form of address in his strong South African accent for most of his pals — "the draw's the shot for me. Always has been, always will be."

I grinned back at him.

"Bobby, you won't do it because you *can't* do it, so I win — a free putting lesson."

I recall Locke sighing at the impudence of this ink-stained wretch as the green cleared, then staring at it for a long beat. Finally, after going to his bag and selecting a long-iron, he set up, it seemed, as always with all parts of him in their usual draw-producing positions, then made what appeared to be his usual fluid but way-inside-to-out, roly-poly draw swing. Certain I was about to witness that shape of shot, I watched in true amazement as the ball soared into a beautiful high fade that seemed to descend feather-like, before hitting the green softly, rolling briefly, and stopping a few feet from the hole.

Grinning broadly, Locke walked over and put an arm around my shoulders as he murmured, "Maarstah, that Pabst is going to taste *specially* good today. And what a singsong we'll have."

One person who was distinctly unimpressed with Arthur d'Arcy Locke's golf game when the South African showed up in the U.S. for the first time was the legendary Ben Hogan, who, among other criticisms, apparently commented to some fellow players that Bobby's left-hand grip was too weak for him ever to become successful on America's long tour courses.

Hearing about the comment, Locke was reported to have provided one of the game's all-time most pithy responses: "Maarstah, if that's true, it's just fine. Because at the presentations I take the checks with my right hand."

Sadly, Bobby Locke's final years were impaired by the ever-worsening affects of severe head and leg injuries suffered when he was hit by a train while riding in a car as a passenger, three days after the birth of his only child, a daughter. He also incurred some legal problems, including arrest for drunk driving, and a three-month suspended sentence for shooting and wounding a native laborer with whom he had gotten into a dispute. He died in the late 1980s of spinal meningitis, and his wife and daughter committed suicide together in 2001.

It was no storybook ending, but for those who knew him at his finest—or even just watched him—there will never be another Arthur d'Arcy "Bobby" Locke.

eleven

SEÑOR MAGICAL
MERCURIAL

Severiano Ballesteros was the most mercurial superstar golfer I ever encountered: fun to be around in his upbeat moods, and various categories of a pain in the butt when the blues hit home. And, at least in my years of our acquaintanceship, the worst element of dealing with him was never knowing which personality would show up—or when a sudden about-face might occur.

Nevertheless, along with many of the golf world's power-brokers Ballesteros periodically enraged, his magical playing skills and achievements during his peak years (87 victories worldwide including five majors), his exceptional good looks and physical "presence," and his off-beat approach to many aspects of life, including golf, made serious umbrage with him difficult to sustain.

Fellow Hispanic Lee Trevino—not surprisingly, a good friend of and periodic counselor to Seve—will always for me be the game's supreme self-taught superstar of my era, but Ballesteros comes a close second. And that, I've long sadly believed, has been his undoing, as attempting to swing "mechanically" via a succession of instructors after his instinctive abilities began waning compounded diving confidence with ever-increasing "method" confusion. Sadly, he played just once on the U.S. over-50 (Champions) tour, but, after finishing last, quickly announced his retirement from tournament golf.

Most authorities agree that since his last win—the 1995 Spanish Open—Seve's primary problem has been with the driver, with which Tiger Woods's latest teacher, Hank Haney, believes Ballesteros has developed an extreme case of the "yips" (as did Haney before managing to cure himself). Also, a divorce in 2005 after 16 years of marriage to the daughter of one of Spain's wealthiest men, involving distancing from their children, obviously hasn't helped Ballesteros's psyche.

Regardless of his long and sad competitive decline, however, two of the man's most powerful characteristics particularly stick with me. One is his compulsiveness, the other his unmatched shot-making inventiveness.

Seve played in a number of the TV events I coproduced with the BBC, including twice in our pro-celebrity series (*see page 156*). At a Turnberry series, rather than ride up to the hotel in a limo, his habit after each match was to climb its famous 40 or so steps from the course while bouncing a ball on the face of a wedge as he traversed each one. Often he'd complete the feat successfully, but what really blew everyone away was what happened when he didn't. Back he would hustle to the bottom of the steps, there to start all over again. And then, if necessary, again and again until perfection was achieved.

During that same week, after losing serious sterling to Sean Connery through appalling putting, I asked Seve shortly before dinner one evening if he would take a quick look at my ailing action. Out we went to the resort's par-3 course, where we remained until he—regardless of my ever-growing antsiness—had become 100 percent assured that I had not only fully grasped his instructions mentally, but was executing them perfectly physically. Which made both of us extremely late eating dinner!

Many of Ballesteros's peak-time opponents will vouch for his incredible ability to invent and execute unorthodox golf shots. Here's my favorite example.

The Spanish ace was practicing from a greenside bunker ahead of the 1994 U.S. Open at Oakmont when Jack Nicklaus and Ben Crenshaw showed up to do the same. After watching them for a few moments, Seve sidled over, grinned, and said, "I play you both for $1 closest to hole," whereupon he upends the club he's been using to show them that it's a 3 iron. Momentarily puzzled, Jack and Ben both stared at the long-iron head, then looked at the sand wedges in their hands. Finally, they raised their eyebrows to each other, grinned broadly, and nodded their agreement to what seemed like a sure thing.

Going first, Nicklaus blasted a ball to within a couple of feet of the cup, followed by Crenshaw, who got just inside him. Smiling, Seve nodded congratulations, then, crouching low to facilitate addressing the ball way outside his left foot and opening the 3 iron's blade until it faced the sky, he made a soft little swing that lofted the ball to within a few feet of the hole, from where it ran to hang on the lip.

I can't recall ever seeing a couple of big-time sports figures look as stunned as Jack and Ben at that moment. When, after a moment, Ballesteros—his expression a picture of innocence—inquired, "Again?" both quickly declined.

But for me the greatest example of the Spaniard's phenomenal self-taught shot-making ability was the greatest play I've ever witnessed—and good fortune has allowed me to watch all of the greats from the Palmer-Nicklaus-Player "Big Three" heroics to the present day. That shot occurred in the 1983 Ryder Cup match at PGA National in Palm Beach Gardens, Florida, and was followed by another exceptional play when Lanny Wadkins hit a 60-yard pitch to within a foot of the hole for birdie to halve with Jose Maria Olazabal, giving the U.S. a one-point win—and possibly saving first-time captain Nicklaus from a heart attack!

Fine as Wadkins's play was, however, it seemed almost routine compared to Seve's a little earlier. Using an old, tiny-headed Toney Penna 3 wood and hitting from a severe uphill and side-hill lie from near the steep forward lip of a fairway bunker at the final hole, a par-5, the Spaniard flew his ball 240 yards to the back fringe of the green, from where he got up and down for birdie to tie his match against Fuzzy Zoeller.

Nicklaus later commented that he also had never seen a greater shot.

Severiano Ballesteros may have become one of the saddest cases in the saga of star-golfer declines, but no one in the game's history produced more gallery amazement and excitement during his prime years. Nor, in my view, has any player done more to raise modern European professional playing standards and aspirations.

So every time the Euros win the Ryder Cup—as at the time of writing they had done five out of the last six playings—tip your hat to Señor Magical Mercurial.

twelve

"IT WAS GENIUS"

No passing of a great golfer in my lifetime generated a greater or warmer outpouring of tributes from around the world than John Byron Nelson's.

To my mind, the reason for that is encapsulated in this repeat of a tribute quoted earlier from Minister Rick Atchley's eulogy to "Lord Byron" at his funeral service, attended by some 2,500 friends and admirers following his death at age 93 in late 2006: "We can debate over which man was the greatest golfer, but there is no debate over which golfer was the greatest man."

Perhaps because he quit regular competition at the peak of his powers while still a young man to fulfill his dream of becoming a rancher, Nelson, despite his incredible record, never to my mind received quite the level of recognition he merited, and especially in terms of his impact on swing technique. I believe the following three epiphanies catch its essence.

First, Jack Nicklaus's only hosannah to another player's technique in his autobiography, *My Story*:

> It was said of the great English champion Harry Vardon that he never wanted to play the same course twice in one day because he was so accurate that he would have been hitting in the second round from the divot marks he made in the first.
>
> Harry Vardon died three years before I was born, but I can't believe he was any more accurate than the golfer who gave a clinic during the U.S. Junior Championship at the Los Angeles Country Club in August of 1954. There was a new irrigation system in the fairway where he was hitting, and I'll never forget sitting with other kids watching shot after shot, with all the clubs, drop smack on the line where the center piping

was laid. It was incredible…awesome, as they say today…and still the finest exhibition of golfing accuracy I've ever witnessed.

And, of course, Nelson at that time was 42 years old and long retired as a full-time tournament player.

Few golf teachers have achieved the eminence and respect enjoyed by America's Bob Toski and Britain's John Jacobs, each following years of successful tournament play. Here are their epiphanies from a *Golf World* appreciation of Nelson by, in my opinion, the game's current finest writer, Jaime Diaz (reproduced with his permission):

> "I loved to watch him, because he did it with such ease," says [Toski]. "Over the ball, he was always in motion, so in tune with his body. When he played golf, Byron looked like he was dancing."
>
> Toski remembers in particular a mid-1950s practice session with Nelson at Cypress Point G.C. "We were on the practice tee at the Crosby…and I asked him to hit some drivers off the fairway. Now Byron was famous for hitting a straight ball, but he said, 'What would you have me do?' So I called out 'low fade,' 'high fade,' 'low straight,' 'high straight,' 'low draw,' and finally, 'high draw.'
>
> "He hit every single one with the correct shape and right on the screws. He paused before the last one to tell me, 'Now, this one's the hardest,' and then just painted a soft draw against the sky. I said, 'Byron, that was unbelievable,' and he took my open palm and put it against his. He had huge, very thick hands. 'Bob,' he said, 'look at the difference. I can hit all those shots because I have the strength and feel in my hands to control the club and the direction of the clubface. I was blessed.'"

And, finally, Jacobs: "Byron was upright away from the ball—very straight back and a bit steep—but he matched it with compensatory knee flex coming down that made his hitting area very long and very flat. That combination of actions was better than orthodox, almost beyond technique. You could never teach it. It was genius."

Any time you catch it on the screws and fly it absolutely dead straight with your 21st-century swing, give a nod to "Lord Byron."

thirteen

GOOD FOR THE KIDNEYS

Regarding him with so many others as golf's supreme gentleman-player, Byron Nelson was one of the two people I never failed to seek out in all my early years of covering the Masters. The other was Gene Sarazen, one of the smallest of the greats, but also almost certainly, in his prime, the feistiest. In good weather, both men would spend many hours sitting just outside the rear of the Augusta National clubhouse overlooking the patio and its famed oak tree, where they would happily chat with just about anyone who cared to stop by.

Nelson was such a good-natured and easygoing individual that, for me, just being around him and listening to him talk, regardless of the subject, had a tonic effect in that early April hotbed of monster egos and self-preoccupation.

Sarazen also loved to recall golf's past and its personalities, usually in more anecdotal fashion. And, even though much mellowed by then, his hackles would still occasionally rise about a rival or a competitive experience, giving one the sense that more of his contemporaries were intimidated by him than he was by them, despite his modest build.

And recalling a very different occasion with Gene still makes me chuckle.

My wife and I had reached the 10th tee of Sarazen's then home-course in southwestern Florida when he arrived in a cart as we were about to hit our drives and asked if he might join us for the back nine. A near-beginner at the time, with a hefty handicap, Jean blanched dead white at the request and clearly was severely intimidated. But, of course, there was no way I was going tell the first man to win all four of golf's major championships, and an old friend, to get lost.

To hopefully make my wife more comfortable, before we set off I moved my bag to Gene's cart so that she could miss out a hole or pick up her ball without interfering with our play. Sensing her discomfort, however, Sarazen could not have been more patient or charming, and even ended up offering her some simple tips.

The really stunning moment for me, however, arrived when he encountered a lengthy stretch of severely rutted pathway bordering one of the fairways. With a "Hang on tight" as he headed for them, Sarazen — then well into his seventies — drove the cart the length of the ruts as fast as it would go, causing both of us to shake furiously up and down and from side to side.

Once we reached smooth passage again, I exclaimed, "Wow! What was *that* all about?"

"Don't you know?" he said with a grin. "A really good body shaking is just great for the kidneys. Done it every time I've had the chance, so never had any kidney problems."

He didn't seem to have many problems with his golf game, either, shooting just 1 over par for the nine holes.

fourteen

MR. GENEROSITY

And then there was the case of Willie and the Slammer...
Although never a fan of links golf, Samuel Jackson Snead showed up
for the British Open at Royal Troon in 1962, having been persuaded to
promote by his presence at that championship the interests of his lifelong
club maker, the Wilson Sporting Goods Company, concomitant with the
opening of its first European plant in a nearby town. Snead had, of
course, won the title at St. Andrews in 1946, despite considering the
course little more than a goat track—that after finishing ninth at
Carnoustie, which he also disliked, in his first and only previous attempt
in 1937.

As is customary with most players and caddies on most longer links
holes, due to the severity of the trouble lining their fairways, Sam's bag-
man would hand him his driver as they came off the previous green, then
make his way well down the hole in order, hopefully, to be close enough
to the vicinity of the tee shot's landing area to easily locate the ball.

Seemingly unhappy with life in general and his game in particular, in
his opening practice round, following an unusually wild drive, Sam simply let the club fall to the tee over his shoulder, then left it there as, mut-
tering to himself, he strutted up the fairway. Which, of course, meant that
his caddie—by then almost 300 yards away—would have to return to the
tee to retrieve the club, then repeat the trek he'd already made in doing
his job correctly.

But Willie—as later I learned was his name—had a surprise in store
for the legendary American.

Wordlessly and expressionlessly, Willie gently laid Sam's bag where
he'd been awaiting the golfer, then marched smartly back to the tee.
Upon arriving there, he picked up the offending club, but instead of

immediately heading back up the fairway with it, he stood and waved it at Sam, as though indicating, "Okay, I got it, and I'll be back with it in a jiffy."

However, once he was sure he had Snead's full attention, Willie's next move was to swing the club in an ever-faster circling motion above his head, until, letting it go, he whirlygigged the thing a good 50 or 60 yards deep into some tall weeds. This, not unnaturally given the circumstances, inspired most of the onlookers to give him a hearty round of applause. Having bowed appreciatively to them, Willie turned to wave once more at his erstwhile employer, then spun on his heels and headed for the clubhouse.

Fortunately for the Slammer, a spectator volunteered to retrieve the club and then carry the bag for the rest of the round, and did well enough for Sam to hire him for the championship. At age 50, Snead tied for fifth, 16 shots behind a rampaging Arnold Palmer, and afterward I asked his volunteer caddie how much he'd been paid.

"Och aye, he was verra kind," came the response. "He gave me a five-pund note after each round, then a dozen new golf balls from his locker at the end."

Mr. Generosity himself!

fifteen

No More Great Rivalries?

Great rivalries have been one of the most entertaining aspects of professional tournament golf throughout most of its history. But could that phenomena be over?

Beginning with the "Great Triumvirate" of Harry Vardon versus J.H. Taylor versus James Braid, the classic battlers have comprised Bobby Jones versus Walter Hagen versus Gene Sarazen; Ben Hogan versus Byron Nelson versus Sam Snead; Jack Nicklaus versus Arnold Palmer versus Gary Player versus Billy Casper; and Jack Nicklaus versus Lee Trevino and Tom Watson.

The biggest rivalry to have materialized in men's golf since Jack versus Tom seems to me to be a fellow called Woods competing primarily against every record in the book. However, until Phil Mickelson collapsed so humiliatingly on the final hole of the 2006 U.S. Open, he appeared well on his way to evolving into a solid adversary for Tiger—and, of course, may still do so. Beyond that possibility, at the time of writing, however, truly great rivalries seem a thing of the past.

Not long ago, each of the one-time "Big Three"—Player, Palmer, and Nicklaus—commented on that sad state of affairs:

Said Player, "I believe too many golfers today are happy to finish second or third. I get so [ticked] off with that. No one but your wife and your dog remember if you finished second—and that's only if you have a good wife and a great dog."

Said Palmer, "Until other players [than Woods] start winning majors on a consistent basis, golf will continue to lack great rivalries. Blame the comfortable living that the game today can provide even middling pros.

For instance, I recall Tiger got $1 million for winning his first U.S. Open. Well, the *total* prize money my first year on tour [1954] was $750,000. So, if you weren't in the top one or two, in a couple of years you were back home mining coal."

Said Nicklaus: "Regardless of money or titles, Tiger's hunger to win is such that, given good health, he will never, ever stop trying to get better. The problem with most of those competing against him presently is that their hunger decreases the more comfortable they become financially, which is easier and easier to achieve as purses keep escalating."

It seems to me that two problems especially impact the prize money and thereby the incentive factor.

First, I believe an "entitlement" mentality pervades today's PGA Tour, meaning that "good" as opposed to "great" players believe all the sweat and toil and time they've put into the game gives them a *right* to become wealthy by playing it, regardless of winning or losing.

Second, the compensation levels of the people running the show depend more than anything else on continually increasing purses to benefit all levels of player, which inevitably feeds the above mentality. (And, boy, just imagine how popular that observation will make me at the tour's headquarters in Ponte Vedra!)

sixteen

"The Stupid Nature
of the Idiot Game"

America is a nation in which sports success, once achieved, must at best be constantly elevated, or at worst sustained, for the perpetrator to avoid severe second-guessing or at least temporary slippage in star quotient.

Golf is particularly susceptible to this syndrome.

Here's one example:

Deriving from media hubbub—including masses of "it's-over" type write-offs—whenever he went more than few months without winning a major, the greatest player in history saw fit to write in his autobiography, *My Story*, not one but two long chapters addressing the question, "What's Wrong with Jack Nicklaus?"

Here's another.

Tiger Woods's "only" tying for third in the Masters then missing the U.S. Open cut at Winged Foot in 2006—despite the long illness and finally the death a few weeks previously of his beloved father, best friend, and primary mentor—produced torrents of print and screen speculation about, at best, "A slump," and, at worst, the "Is he done?" question. By the end of the year, of course, Woods had won his third British Open, his third PGA Championship, nine out his 20 tournament starts, and been named world "Sportsman of the Year" by *Sports Illustrated*.

The truth, of course, is that all such downbeat ink and chatter demonstrates ignorance or avoidance of the harsh realities of golfing "form." Fortunately, for those with the interest and energy, a careful study of the game's past—by clearly defining its patterns of success and failure—sharply illuminates its two greatest conundrums.

Don't want to go to that much trouble? Fine, here they are:

Conundrum number one is that playing form, even at the highest levels of skill, dedication, and desire, is always ephemeral, meaning that peak performance at golf is sustainable only for relatively brief periods of time. In other words, just like recreational players, for short spells—usually at most from a few days to a few weeks—the stars, having found "IT," are able to keep "IT." But then—generally quite suddenly and for no immediately discernible reason—all or part of "IT" just vanishes into the blue.

Perhaps the primary cause of that, at every level of golf, is simply overdoing whatever worked so well for a while.

Another is what I think Bernard Darwin, golf's earliest doyen of writers and himself a good player, in one of his many rages of frustration over sudden loss of form, labeled simply, "The stupid nature of the idiot game."

Just as unmanageable, of course, is conundrum number two, being that attaining peak form at any particular time for any given occasion, no matter how much desire and effort goes into the attempt, is comparably volatile. Or, in other words, in golf, luck or happenstance frequently plays more of a role than desire or effort in attaining performance peaks.

Thus, if these arguments are sound, striving and struggling as Jack did, and Tiger surely still does, to become 100 percent "ready" for any particular tournament—and especially those four very special weeks of the major championships each year—is and always will be as much a matter of pot luck as toil, sweat, and fiery desire. Sure, those and other qualities must be part of the mix, but all too often they will prove in vain.

So is it truly a sign that the end is nigh, or even that just a "slump" has inexplicably occurred, when golfers of the highest caliber fail when they have striven their hardest to succeed?

Not in my book.

All that's distressing and humbling them is the eternal and ineradicable fickleness of attaining, then holding, top form at golf over any given period of time.

Making the answer to "What's wrong with —?": "Hey, just give 'em time, and happenstance—mixed with effort, of course—will bring 'em back."

seventeen

MAJOR CHAMPIONSHIP QUIZ

Surely there cannot be a golfer on this planet who doesn't know who holds what inarguably is the game's supreme record: winner of most professional major championships. And I'd guess very few are unaware how fast another guy is closing in on that phenomenal total.

As a reminder, however, the names respectively are Jack William Nicklaus, with 18 major victories, but now retired from competition; and Eldrick "Tiger" Woods with 13 at the time of writing, and assumedly many fine competitive years ahead of him.

What probably even the game's most dedicated stats nerds couldn't answer without consulting a record book, however, is how many golfers since the first British Open was played at Prestwick in 1860 have won at least two of the four biggies—the other three being, of course, the Masters, the U.S. Open, and the PGA Championship.

I happened on that number in a cleverly compiled column in the *New York Times* the day after Mr. Woods notched his 13th major victory in a week of 100-degree-plus heat at Tulsa's Southern Hills in August of 2007, just 11 seasons after turning pro. Studying it provoked me into offering the following teasers (*answers on page 64*):

1. An easy one to start: How many players won all four majors at least once, and who are they?

2. Only three players have attained double figures in majors victories. Nicklaus and Woods are, of course, the two leaders. Who's number three?

3. How many of the eight golfers who won between seven and nine professional majors apiece are still alive? And who are they?

4. Bobby Jones, the game's all-time greatest amateur, won 13 events considered majors in his day. In how many of them did he defeat the world's best pros?

5. Who has won the most (a) Masters, (b) U.S. Opens, (c) British Opens, (d) PGA Championships?

6. How many non-American-born players won two or more majors?

7. In which country were the most non-American-born majors winners born? And how many Big Four victories have they amassed?

8. Which two non-American-born brothers won three U.S. Opens between them?

9. English is not the native tongue of only four multiple major championship winners. What is the language of two with seven victories between them and the most letters in their names?

10. How many golfers in the game's history have won two or more major championships?

Answers to Major Championship Quiz (from previous page)

1. Five: Jack Nicklaus, Tiger Woods, Gary Player, Ben Hogan, and Gene Sarazen.
2. Walter Hagen with 11 (two U.S. Opens, four British Opens, five PGAs).
3. Three: Gary Player, Tom Watson, Arnold Palmer. (Deceased: Ben Hogan, Bobby Jones, Gene Sarazen, Sam Snead, and Harry Vardon.)
4. Jones won four U.S. Opens and three British Opens, defeating the world's top pros. His other victories then considered majors consisted of five U.S. Amateurs and one British Amateur.
5. Masters: Jack Nicklaus (6). U.S. Open: Jack Nicklaus (4), Ben Hogan (4), Bobby Jones (4), Willie Anderson (4). British Open: Harry Vardon (6). PGA Championship: Jack Nicklaus (5), Walter Hagen (5).
6. Thirty-four (although a handful became naturalized Americans).
7. The United Kingdom (17), mostly a century or more ago. Of modern times, Australia and South Africa are tied second with four each.
8. Carnoustie, Scotland–born Alex and Willie Smith.
9. Spanish (Severiano Ballesteros and Jose Maria Olazabal).
10. Seventy-four (40 being Americans by birth).

part two

TECHNIQUE

eighteen

AT LAST!

It was a mid-afternoon in August, the temperature close to 100, the humidity appalling.

There was only one person at the pit-like bottom of our range, one of our club's oldest and most gentlemanly members, a distinguished New York lawyer by then retired. Slumped on a bench, sweat-soaked, pasty-faced, and looking about ready to pass out, clearly he'd been hitting balls—and, given the weather conditions, too many balls for a man well into his eighties.

Hustling up in my cart, I asked him, "Charlie, are you *okay?* Because you sure don't look too good. Do you need help?"

Charlie somehow produced the vestige of a grin.

"No," he semi-whispered, "I'll be all right. I just started feeling a little faint so decided to rest for a bit. I'll be fine in a few moments."

Then, mopping his dripping face with a towel and sitting up straighter, he smiled broadly and added the few words that I think typifies the addiction known as golf better than anything I've heard:

"But, you know, I really do think I've finally GOT IT!"

nineteen

A FORM OF MASOCHISM!

L ast time I checked, the average handicap of American male golfers was 19, meaning that breaking 100 represented a really good day. Women players' average handicap was then 26, meaning they bumped it around in 100-plus far more often than not.

Why so "bad"?

Not least because of its cost in money and time, recreational players mostly take up golf relatively late in life. As a result, few by then possess the strength, flexibility, dexterity, energy, patience, and time—or all six— to develop first-rate playing skills.

Or, in short, the vast majority of golfers worldwide are doomed by their late starts to remain for life what good players disparagingly regard— mostly privately—as "hackers" or "choppers."

Another contributing factor to the general ineptitude is that so many beginning adults, of whatever age, either try to learn by hit and miss as they play, or take advice from well-meaning but unschooled friends who more often than not exacerbate their difficulties. The moral of which, of course, is to get lessons from a qualified instructor before you have time to ingrain a multitude of faults.

I've always felt incompetence at the game is largely why certain types of people try to con their fellows that they play primarily for fresh air, or exercise, or companionship, rather than for the true reason: the incurable addiction they've developed for golf despite how severely it punishes them.

In other words, the darn game is a primary form of masochism!

twenty

SEARCHING FOR GOLF'S HOLY GRAIL

Tiger Woods's lifelong multiplicity of instructors, and seemingly endless intensity of coaching even as he dominates the game, clearly has done him vastly more good than harm. Jack Nicklaus, on the other hand, got most of what he learned about technique as a youngster from a single teacher named Jack Grout, who thereafter did more heartening and reassuring of the Bear than "mechanical" fiddling.

So how about the "normal" mortal?

Well, consider the following…

I have a pal—who also happens to be one of Nicklaus's oldest friends—who emigrated to America from Macedonia at age 12 without a word of English; learned the language quickly and well enough to excel in high school; served with distinction as a Marine in World War II; quarterbacked Ohio State to a famous Rose Bowl victory; launched, ran, and eventually made a fortune selling a safety-equipment business; and served a 30 year spell as general chairman of Nicklaus's Memorial Tournament. But, exceptional as those achievements are, to his best buddies, none are Pandel Savic's primary distinction.

Rather, his most remarkable achievement in life is having taken what is believed to be more golf lessons than anyone in the game's 600-plus-year history!

Unprovable as that assumption is, here's perhaps the best example of what created and sustains it.

Pandel once began a bright and shiny day at his Florida club by taking an early morning lesson from the resident teaching professional. Having then scored less than satisfactorily in the ensuing round, following lunch he persuaded his partner—renowned Midwestern instructor Rick Jones, who happened to be visiting—to provide another lengthy tutorial session. When that appeared not to have fully "taken" after another lengthy spell of solo range work, Savic finally tracked down Gardner Dickinson, the tour-pro-turned-teaching-ace who was also a member of the club, for a third session.

Inevitably, all three instructors identified different faults and offered different fixes, leaving Pandel not only exhausted but doing a lot of head scratching.

Over the years, Nicklaus was among those who enjoyed much good-natured bantering about his great friend's relentless quest for what he called the "Holy Grail" of golf. Frequently, Jack would explain to another of their pals that the search had led Savic to not really play the game they and he did, but rather one called "Golf Swing."

Regardless of all the ribbing, Pandel finally decided he would write a book based on the multitude of notes he had made from his experiences. Aptly enough, it would be called, *I Never Had a Lesson I Didn't Like: The Search for Golf's Holy Grail*.

Amusing? Undoubtedly.

But the real moral of this story seems to me to be that Pandel Savic played to a low single-figure handicap for more than 50 years, and was still doing so—and still searching—as he entered his ninth decade.

Indicating, wouldn't you say, that too much instruction is better than not enough?

twenty-one

WORKING WITH
BRITAIN'S
"DOCTOR GOLF"

Getting to work over many years with John Jacobs, Britain's legendary "Doctor Golf," was one of my most enjoyable experiences in life its ownself (cheers again, Dan Jenkins!).

John and I ended up doing hundreds of magazine pieces, four books, and a number of videos—all instructional, but especially challenging for the writer/producer in that "J.J.'s" teaching was entirely "non-mechanical," meaning that it required defining, describing, and depicting "feels" and motions rather than the "positional" factors involved in swinging a golf club.

Initially a tournament professional good enough to make Britain and Ireland's Ryder Cup team (he defeated Cary Middlecoff in the 1953 singles), Jacobs, following competitive retirement, added founding, developing, and for some years running the European Tour to his instructional efforts.

How good a teacher was "Doctor Golf" in the flesh?

For a short spell I ran a golf center named for him near London. There, I'd watch with amazement as he worked with raw beginners—some straight off the trucks they drove or the brick walls they laid for a living—and have them hitting nice little draws with short irons within minutes of stopping by their driving-range booths.

And then, because he taught entirely from what the ball's flight imparted about impact "geometry," there was his stunning ability to fix regular pupils' problems—even up to Walker Cup–player level—via telephone conversation.

"How're you missing it?" he'd ask. "What 'shape' mostly?" Then, once told, "Ahhh! Well, if you…" And the diagnosis rarely took him more than a minute or two, either.

Tiger Woods's latest teacher, Hank Haney, studied under and remains a great believer in many of J.J.'s approaches. And longtime number one in top golf magazine instructor rankings, Butch Harmon (who previously worked with Tiger), is also a fan of Jacobs. Perhaps most impressive of all, Sam Snead once told me he'd learned more from listening to John expound on technique at *Golf Digest* teaching seminars than from any other external source.

Also, through 2006 Jacobs was one of only two teachers—and the only foreign instructor—inducted into America's World Golf Hall of Fame (the other is legendary Texan Harvey Penick).

An imposing man physically, Jacobs was also the least verbally reticent teacher I ever encountered. Three of his remarks I best remember were:

- To a beginner contacting only air: "All right, madam, you've got it [the ball] scared. Now *hit* it for me."
- To a major American tycoon: "You're swinging *up* at the ball, sir, which doesn't work. So how about taking a little bit of California for me?"
- To a pompous and argumentative British royal: "Sir, you are wasting your money and my time. So I propose we stop immediately."

At least for beginners, of all the instructional books I've worked on — 18 at last count—I'd guess Jacobs's best-selling *Practical Golf* has helped the most players, and especially beginners and high handicappers. In fact, an American teaching peer of John's once said to me, "Anyone who reads that book's first three chapters knows all they will ever need to about hitting a golf ball."

And if you take that as a plug, fine!

twenty-two

"MIGHTY MOUSE"

In my days of editing *Golf Digest* magazine back in the early 1970s, I brought Bob Toski to its Connecticut offices to sign the diminutive one-time tour star and, later, longtime legendary instructor, as a contributor. The magazine's "how-to" panel in those days was top-heavy with former tour players with high "name" value but limited teaching experience, and Toski was number one on my recruiting list to switch that balance to favor ace instructors.

We completed our business in the morning, so decided to fill the lovely spring afternoon by eating lunch and playing golf at my Connecticut club, no pushover from the back tees. Having traveled light from his Florida home, Toski had to borrow a set of clubs, and, being so small — Sam Snead in Bob's tour days rechristened the 125-pounder "Mighty Mouse"—he had no choice but to play in street shoes when we couldn't find a pair of spikes to fit him. My predecessor as editor at *Golf Digest*, the late Dick Aultman, also a Toski pal and fan, decided to join us.

This was Bob's first sight of our course. Playing from the tips with the borrowed clubs, in his wing-tips and dress shirt, what would you guess Mighty Mouse shot? The answer is 67.

A member who toasted Mouse's achievement in the bar after the round hit it right on the nose: "Once a player, always a player."

You think "body action" is the key to hitting a golf ball?

Watching Bob Toski hit 4 woods while sitting in a chair might have changed your mind. In his fifties, such shots mostly flew at least 200 yards—and invariably with a gorgeous little draw. By the time he reached his mid-seventies, he'd lost maybe 10 of those yards—but not the draw!

In "Mouse's" mind, it all came down to "effortless power" as opposed to "powerless effort." In mine, it was about a superb pair of hands, plus more than a touch of innate genius.

Because he loved it so much, the Mouse's mood when teaching was mostly relaxed and amiable, with frequent appearances of a sort of lopsided sly smile that his female clients were crazy about. But a certain type of pupil could turn him in the blink of an eye from Dr. Jekyll into Mr. Hyde.

All it took was a man who thought he knew more about the golf swing than any instructor did, and accordingly questioned most of what he was hearing, especially if he'd flown in for the session in a private jet, insisted on staying in the best local hotel's penthouse suite, hit balls wearing a diamond-studded Rolex, but swung like a blind person trying to swat a fly.

The worst explosion I ever witnessed came at one of the first group golf schools that Aultman and I originated and ran for *Golf Digest* way back in our days of editing the magazine.

It was a beautiful morning at a gorgeous resort, and things had proceeded peacefully enough as, for the first time, Toski worked his way down the line of mostly highly impressed, eager, and compliant students. And then, right out of nowhere, I became aware, as overseer, of two steadily rising voices—the Mouse's and an overweight, expensively dressed, increasingly red-faced middle-aged man Bob had shortly before begun teaching. As I watched, the guy, leaning on a club with one hand, wagged a finger of the other in Toski's face, to the point eventually of accidentally tipping the trademark white Hogan-type cap Mouse always wore over his by then blazing eyes.

The only way to describe our man's reaction, as he righted the cap and bellied up to the guy—who must have weighed twice what he did—was that he "lost it," and I mean totally.

After kicking away the club the fellow was leaning on so that he almost fell over, Mouse ripped the man's elegant straw Fedora off his head, tossed it on the ground between them into a mess of divot dirt, then jumped up and down on it with both feet until it could have passed for an extremely ill-abused pie-crust.

Hurrying over to "referee," so to speak, I heard "moron" and "idiot" come across loud and clear, along with the Mouse's instruction, as I drew closer, that the pupil gather his clubs and his "stupid" tour-size golf bag, remove himself from the range as fast as possible, race to the airport, instantly depart in his jet, and be sure never again—on pain of even more severe assault—to come within sight or sound of our senior instructor. Oh, and before he did all that, here was the crux of the only lesson he deserved: immediately give up any further attempts to play golf, which game was clearly way beyond both his intellectual and physical capacity, even if his oversize and out-of-shape body could bear the stress of beating the blankety blank thing around in the high 100s—which was definitely the lowest he was ever going to score.

Phew!

With the now puce-faced pupil doing more or less as instructed, I somehow managed to propel the still enraged senior instructor into the club's grill room, where eventually he calmed down enough to tell me one of the dirtiest jokes I've ever heard.

And the even better news was that, for the rest of that "trial" school week, there were absolutely no arguments from any of the remaining pupils.

twenty-three

"ONE AND INDIVISIBLE"

Percy Boomer's book, *On Learning Golf*, published in 1942 after 35 years as a teaching professional, is widely regarded as a seminal contribution to swing methodology and instructional literature. I believe all of its various editions are presently out of print, but if you get the chance to obtain an old copy, grab it. I have one and still periodically seek succor from it when my game goes south.

Boomer was born in the village of Grouville on the Channel Island of Jersey in 1884, where his schoolteacher father's charges included the great British champions Harry Vardon and Ted Ray. Boomer's younger brother and star pupil, Aubrey, won 10 European national championships between 1921 and 1932, in addition to tying for second in the 1927 British Open behind Bob Jones.

Deriving from his insistence that players learn to pivot from their hips as the swing's initiating move, Boomer is best remembered as the "turn-in-a-barrel" advocate. And, in keeping with his resolutely non-mechanical approach to the game, he was wonderfully visceral about how to do that, writing simply: "[Imagine] that you are standing in a barrel hip high and big enough to be just free of each hip, but close enough to allow no movement except the pivot."

But perhaps his most profound—and representative—statement was the following: "The only way in which we can repeat correct shots time after time—and this is the greatest of golfing assets—is to be able to repeat the correct *feel* of how they are produced."

Boomer had a long and close association with top golfers, taught for decades, and made a lifelong study of golf's mind-body relationship. The result was a conviction that the easiest route to playing well is via learning and ingraining the *feelings* of the movements that produce good shots, then simply replicating them over and over and over, with as little modification for non-routine plays as possible.

Here's his philosophy in a nutshell:

1. Every good golf shot is the product of a satisfactory psychological-physical relationship.
2. It is this relationship which gives control and consistency.
3. These good relationships (and consequent controls) are built up most easily and firmly when the muscular-mechanical requirements of the game have been simplified.

And so—

4. It is desirable to learn to play as many of the shots as possible with the same movements.

Of necessity, Boomer did cover the mechanics of swing motions in both his face-to-face teaching and his book, but always as simply as possible consistent with comprehensibility. Here, for example, is his listing of what he considered the key moves of the basic golf swing:

1. It is essential to turn the body around to the right and then back and around to the left, without moving (sideways) either way. In other words, this turning must be from a fixed pivot. [Hence the "barrel" image.]
2. It is essential to keep the left arm at full stretch throughout the swing—through the back swing, the down swing and the follow through.
3. It is essential to allow the wrists to break [cock or hinge] fully back at the top of the swing.
4. It is essential to delay the actual hitting of the ball until as late in the swing as possible.
5. It is essential not to tighten any muscle concerned in the reactive part of the swing (movement above the waist).
6. It is essential to feel and control the swing *as a whole* and not to concentrate on any part of it.

But then, immediately, he goes back to fluidity, flow, and, most important, *feel*:

"In a sense this last point is the most vital. The swing must be considered and felt as a single unity, not as succession of positions or even a succession of movements.

"The swing is one and indivisible."

twenty-four

THE SECRET

I offer these thoughts after spending way too much of my life studying and thinking and writing about golf technique (12 instructional books with just Jack Nicklaus, for goodness sake!).

The good news is that if you persist long enough with golf, ultimately there will arrive a day when—by your standards, and generally completely out of the blue—you play so well that you will decide that you have found The Secret, and thus never again will hack, bash, chop, or slash that infuriating little white pill all over God's glossy green acres. That's happened to me maybe a thousand times.

The bad news is that no matter how often we believe otherwise, you and I—and Tiger Woods, come to that—have *not* found The Secret. The reason is, I've sadly come to accept, is that there ain't no such animal.

The even worse news is that, by desperately trying to replicate whatever you think you did that last euphoric time, you will play even more appallingly than you did previously.

As run-of-the-mill tour pros routinely shooting 65 one day and 75 the next so perfectly exemplify, golf is *imperfectable* by human beings. As touched on previously, the primary reason why, in my opinion, is that—no matter the amount of head work and practice sweat expended—everyone always eventually overdoes whatever he or she decides is the key to the game for them.

But the primary reason, of course, is that *Homo sapiens* have not so far evolved to the point of being able to perform *any* set of motions—much less those as complex and unnatural as required in swinging a golf club effectively—with machine-like precision.

What I do believe contains a shred of truth, however, is the theory that golf's sheer imperfectability is primarily what makes so many mature, intelligent, and otherwise sane and accomplished people throughout the world persist in self-flagellating themselves with the game, in many cases almost from cradle to grave.

To me, this thesis is supported by the fact that, if you delve deeply enough, you will discover that the more successful in other endeavors people are, the more likely they are to suffer from the terrible fallacy that they will some day master golf.

I'm here to tell them that they won't. Or, at least, never totally, and in most cases rarely more than fleetingly.

But, please, don't let that stop you from trying!

twenty-five

PUBLISHED INSTRUCTION: GOLD OR GARBAGE?

Despite the foregoing, deep down, every golfer I know will continue to believe there *is* a "Secret" to the game, and I suspect a great many hope to one day find it in a golf periodical—instructional material being that mini-industry's lifeblood, especially the monthlies.

Certainly my sharpest lesson as an editor regarding instruction's importance from the profit perspective was the drop in both subscribership and newsstand sales when, for periods of a few months, we reduced the "how-to" content of Britain's *Golf World* below 40 percent of each issue. Without a speedy return to at least that level, our diminishing circulation—and, concomitantly, our declining ad revenue—told us we would shortly be able to spend all the time we wanted seeking The Secret because we would be otherwise unemployed.

In that regard, I invariably get a kick out the people—in Britain at least, mostly old-geezerish male members of the more elite clubs—who deride virtually all forms of printed instruction, especially in magazine form. "Never even look at it, old chap," I still repeatedly hear in my subconscious from my *Golf World* days. "It's all total garbage."

Occasionally, I asked such people how they knew the stuff was useless if they never read it. The answer, invariably, contained sufficient bluster to suggest that the complainer had, indeed, absorbed every word and pored over every illustration, but then—having been unable to put whatever was advised into beneficial effect on the range or course—had decided out of sheer frustration or disappointment that it was, at best, a waste of space or, at worst, pure claptrap.

So why then, I would ask myself, did such golfers keep on buying golf magazines crammed with such material? And the answer, of course, was simply that old cliché: hope springs eternal in the human breast. Meaning that even the pooh-poohers were still prepared to gamble on something someday appearing that magically turned them from a 20-handicapper into a 12, or even—miracle of miracles!—ultimately a 2.

At the other end of the scale, of course, are the readers who adore instructional material so much that they write editors gushing letters, detailing the swing and/or scoring improvement(s) they've derived from particular articles, and pleading that the staff keep piling it on so they can advance their games even further.

As a form of market research, when editing both *Golf World* and *Golf Digest*, I would occasionally write to such readers after so beneficial a piece had appeared, asking them whether what they'd learned still worked, and, if so, to what extent. My recollection is that a few were ecstatic about how much better players they remained, while about the same percentage were disgruntled by how fast the magic from the "rag" had worn off. The majority replied that the move, or thought, or feel, they'd acquired from the piece had by then largely or entirely evaporated— but requested nevertheless that we keep publishing "how to" because they hoped—indeed, in some cases, even prayed—for more stuff that *might* improve their games, even if only temporarily.

One of the numerous things I learned from this mini-research was that professional teachers—even those who don't themselves play all that well—unquestionably provide more helpful magazine "how-to" material than the great majority of professional players.

Which got me asking myself, why?

Pretty quickly, I reasoned the primary answer was economics.

In other words, quite naturally and rightly, "players" dwell almost entirely on what *they* want and need to do to win titles or moolah or both, whereas teachers will starve fast unless they focus entirely and deeply on what their *pupils* want and need to do.

So, yes, by all means cast your eye over what the world's greats have to offer about playing the game in their invariably brief (and sometimes surprisingly superficial) magazine "takes" on its various technical elements, because some little thing could always click—although invariably temporarily (see previous chapter). But, if it's their level of performance you aspire to, I'd suggest spending most of your time and effort with whatever the best teacher you can find has to offer.

Or, of course, there's always the Ben Hogan alternative: just go dig it out of the dirt alone and unaided.

twenty-six

"Once You've Had 'Em, You've Got 'Em!"

Theoretically, rolling a 1.68-inch-diameter ball into a 4.25-inch-diameter hole over smooth, closely cropped turf from a distance of three or four feet should be a cinch.

In reality, that task becomes immensely difficult, to the point of near impossibility, for the severest sufferers from what have universally come to be known as the "yips."

As a lifelong indifferent-to-horrible putter, I've decided there are essentially three causes of the yips—all, of course, mental.

First is that the seeming physical simplicity of the act of holing a very short putt makes inability to do so highly embarrassing. This, of course, converts the ingrained yipper's mind to jelly and his or her muscles to completely beyond control even as the ball is approached.

The second guaranteed yip-producer is that the psychic distress arising from repeatedly feeling inept and foolish greatly debilitates all future efforts. Or, in short, as the legendary British golf writer/TV commentator Henry Longhurst used to say, "Once you've had 'em, you've got 'em."

But perhaps the overriding problem is the impact of the finality of missing very short putts on both your score and your emotional well-being.

Screw up any other shot in golf and you still have a chance to recover.

Miss a short putt and that stroke is gone, gone, gone forever, forever, forever.

Aaaaaargh!

twenty-seven

GREAT PUPILS
SURE HELP

With some notable exceptions, I've found that most club golf pros tend to teach the swing whichever way they believe they themselves execute it.

Unfortunately, as high-speed photography regularly proves, what even really fine golfers think or feel they do is rarely what's actually happening. And, even when it is, the odds on other people being able to replicate those actions are very low, especially the more athletic and/or practice-intensive the aces are.

Accordingly, the best instructors to my mind are the full-timers whose entire livelihoods depend on somehow being able to get mostly out-of-shape, poorly coordinated, non-practicing amateurs to elevate the ball and send it in approximately the desired direction sufficiently often for them to believe they are having fun with the game.

But, of course, the problem with that is there are, at most, only a few hundred such instructors on the entire planet, compared with the many thousands to whom teaching is just one element of a multifaceted club job.

Perhaps the truest and wisest statement ever made about teaching golf was that of Jack Grout, Jack Nicklaus's lifelong friend and instructor, whenever he was complimented on his contribution to the Golden Bear's achievements.

Among the most modest of men, Grout invariably would reply: "I may be an okay teacher, but it sure does help to have a truly great, great pupil."

twenty-eight

MY BEST-EVER
(TEMPORARY!)
SWING FIX

As even its greatest players have often remarked, golf is a game that one never stops learning.

Case in point: fighting age and some of the minor infirmities that inevitably go with it, my once plus-1 handicap swing had deteriorated to the point where I considered quitting the game. (That would never have happened, of course, but it was the closest I'd come.)

Finally, truly desperate, I managed to obtain a few minutes on a range with friend and longtime ace instructor David Leadbetter. All it took was three or four passes.

"No after-impact extension," said the great man. "Swing the clubhead as far as you can out to the left of the target line, letting your body turn through as you do so. Forget everything else."

There was immediate improvement, but then I played a vacation round in Europe with an ex–tour pro turned teacher. "Any suggestions?" I asked after a couple of sayonara tee shots. He repeated Lead's prescription almost word for word.

Back home, dreaming about that long-ago plus-1, I asked a highly able woman instructor, Kim Verrecchio, to take a look. Again: "Extend on the through-swing! Clubhead out left of target line as body turns through."

And the moral?

So many of us spend so much time being taught and thinking about our grip or setup or backswing mechanics that we pay little if any attention to what we do with the club after the ball is hit—or missed.

Try the fix I got if the game is driving you nuts. It's the briefest I ever had, and the best.

(Of course, as in my case, it won't last anywhere near long enough — the reason being that eventually you'll overdo the move, just as I did.)

twenty-nine

POWER

Whether or not they admit it, a near lifetime in the game has convinced me that every male golfer ever born wants to hit the ball farther, particularly off the tee, and ideally much, *much, MUCH* farther. Indeed, for most young, strong, ultra-macho males, this sometimes seems to have become not only the primary goal of the game, but, when occasionally achieved, its most satisfying accomplishment. Like in— whether voiced or just thought—"Hey, how about *that one*, you bunch of wimps!"

Virtually all of the advances in golf club and ball technology over the years—and particularly recently—have derived from this syndrome, as exemplified by the overwhelming "longer" promises of virtually all of today's driver manufacturer advertising.

Testosterone is, of course, the primary fuel of this frequently score-wrecking urge, especially among younger male players. I imagine many women golfers would also like more power, but experience tells me they would rarely accept it at the cost of higher scorecard numbers.

Here's how to have a little fun with the male basher syndrome.

Find yourself a high-handicap "Mister Universe"–type and watch him strain and drain every muscle in his overdeveloped body attempting to crush the ball into oblivion, only to propel it a fraction of the distance easily achievable by a skilled senior woman player—not to mention thousands of sweet-swinging male Medicare beneficiaries. NFL defensive linemen and competitive weightlifters tend to provide the most giggles, but beware especially of NHL guys—many score extremely well at golf, as well as hitting it mighty long.

If you're power-consumed to the point of getting to hate the game, here are a couple of things to ponder:

1. The more mature, experienced, and successful they became, the more the two greatest golfers in history, Jack Nicklaus and Tiger Woods (who also happened to be, when they needed to be, among the game's all-time longest hitters) favored precision over power. This they achieved, in direct ratio to increasing smarts, by ever more frequently leaving their drivers in the bag on tee shots, in favor of most advantageously positioning the ball with fairway woods and long irons. Of which, of course, the latest great example was Tiger's four rounds of iron-club-only tee shots to avoid ferocious fairway pot bunkers in winning the 2006 British Open at Hoylake.

2. Power in golf is the product of clubhead speed *correctly applied*. If you don't know the meaning of those last two words, rush out and hunt yourself down one of those top-notch teachers referred to earlier.

By the way, I believe the immortally great amateur Bob Jones was the first to explain the why and how of those words in print, and that Britain's "Doctor Golf," John Jacobs, is their supreme modern explicator, especially in *Practical Golf*.

Pitching that book again? Knowing how many people it's helped, you bet!

thirty

IMPROVING

I've long been convinced that, whether they admit it or not, deep down inside, everyone who really sticks with golf desperately wants to improve at the game, if only to reduce the amount of embarrassment and masochistic frustration they so repeatedly inflict upon themselves.

Sadly, even for the few with the physique, conditioning, drive, energy, patience, and opportunity to seriously pursue lasting improvement, achieving it remains a monumental challenge.

Here's my take on why:

Unless, like almost all of golf's great champions over the years, you began at a young age swinging the club effectively—either as a rare "natural" or as the result of ongoing instruction from an expert teacher—you are certain to have ingrained numerous faults in your execution of golf's essential motions. Furthermore, should you simply have tried to pick up the game as you went along, or perhaps taken advice from a relative or pal, the more numerous and damaging those faults are likely to be. Which, of course, leaves you not—as you might be inclined to tell yourself—with simply the challenge of learning to swing the club correctly, but with the equally if not even tougher task of simultaneously "unlearning" the wrongs you've deeply instilled in both your psyche and your muscles.

And the monster hurdle there, of course, is that both eliminating bad moves and mastering correct ones is impossible if you persist, while making the attempt, on playing the course with any thought of scoring effectively. Try that and you will inevitably revert, sooner rather than later, to the inadequate assortment of moves that have plagued you all along, until you again feel at least reasonably physically comfortable attempting to hit a shot. Or, in short, you will go smartly back to your long-ingrained errors.

Thus, what lies ahead of you is practice, and practice only, for weeks, or months, or maybe even years.

Think you might be able to retain your sanity through such an ordeal? Well, here's one way to go about it.

An eventually highly successful British tournament pro friend of mine, recognizing the need to entirely remake his swing, discovered that he was incapable of trying to fix suspected errors whenever he could see the entire flight of a "missed" shot, as on a course or driving range.

Accordingly, for 15 *straight months* and on a daily basis, my pal hit balls only into nets for hour upon hour, thereby eliminating any temptation to depart from his pre-planned regimen through knowing how the ball would have behaved. Relying entirely on the "feel" of impact to tell him how he was progressing, he swears that he never hit a shot outdoors once during that period—but does proudly admit to wearing out the faces of three five irons.

And his reward?

The good news is that he was never incarcerated in a mental institution. The even better news is that he went on to win a fortune over an unusually long and enjoyable pro career.

thirty-one

ON "GIMMES"

A great many of the people I've played non-tournament golf with over the years have been what I call "Gimme Golfers," meaning that "Pick it up" or "That's good" spring frequently to their lips even when everyone else involved—including the puttee—knows the darn thing is of such a length or lie or speed, or all three, as to be highly missable. Should a "giver" be remonstrated with, "saving time" is invariably his or her stated motive. And, indeed, there may be at least a touch of truth to that.

Being a cynic, however, I rarely leave a green where I've been treated over-generously without a suspicion that I will be expected to respond in kind, thereby excusing the "giver" from risking the rage, shame, and embarrassment I invariably feel upon fumbling a shortie.

Another thing that concerns me about accepting a concession of more than say a six-inch "tap-in" is the impact so doing will have on my psyche when suddenly the ball must be holed out. That is, the more I've allowed myself to "pick it up," the greater the pressure I will invariably experience if and when that invitation is not extended, either because the game suddenly is being played for "real" or my opponents have finally become aware of how "yippy" I can get.

Conceding putts of any length is, of course, legal at all levels and forms of match-play golf—contests determined by holes won or lost. In formal head-to-head competition, however, only the shortest of "tap-ins"—of, say, a foot or less—are routinely conceded. When one side is so clearly beyond contending for a hole that requiring it to putt out is meaningless, then longer putts are usually rightly "given."

Conceding putts or accepting concessions in any form of stroke-play tournament—the form of contest determined by totaling strokes played (or points amassed, as in the Stableford format)—is always illegal, with disqualification as the penalty.

The moral of which, of course, is that if one competes seriously at the game, regardless of the stakes, expecting and getting used to knocking the silly little pellet in the stupid little hole is the only way to go.

thirty-two

"IT'S LIKE SEX, OLD BOY"

The great English champion Henry Cotton had yet to be shoulder-tapped by Queen Elizabeth II's ceremonial sword in our many years of closeness, but his knighthood when it came—the first awarded for services to golf—was richly deserved. Not only did this remarkable golfer end a run of 10 straight American victories in the British Open with his first win in 1934, but he captured the old claret jug again in 1937, then, at age 41, for a third time heroically in 1948, along with a long list of other victories.

Of all the top players I've gotten to know, Sir Henry, as he became with the Buckingham Palace ceremony—despite which most of his writer pals still called him "Maestro"—had what in Europe is universally known as "style."

Extensively and elitely educated; a polished speaker; a lively, astute, and prolific writer (nine mostly instructional books and hundreds of columns on golf and life); an epicurean; a fitness fiend; ever perfectly groomed and immaculately garbed; an occasional "society" habitué; and a resident of one of London's choicest West End neighborhoods when not traveling the world with his wealthy Argentinean wife, Toots, Cotton was about as far from the mold of most of his professional contemporaries as it was possible to get. Nor, publicly at least, did he ever give a darn about the envy and jealousy this stirred among some of them.

As, for instance, when doing an exhibition round with a couple of other tournament hotshots, plus the club's pro who couldn't keep it in the ballpark, he loudly inquired of the crowd at one point, "Tell me, someone, would they please? Is this *fellow* actually supposed to be playing with *us?*"

As a golfer, the Maestro was the game's ultimate "hands man," believing and implacably preaching and teaching that strengthening and intensely training those appendages was the best if not by far the only way to shot-making excellence. In his own case—beyond an elegant and effortless-looking overall swinging motion—this produced seemingly magical feats of trick ball-striking. Among them I best remember successions of long and perfectly flighted fairway-wood shots alternately struck with left and right hands alone, plus nonstop driving of 10 or more previously teed balls with zero finger slippage or hand-positioning changes. Invariably, following the amazed applause these feats inspired, they would end with Sir Henry's quiet, "It's all in the hands, you see."

Fascinated by and an immense admirer of the man, I was fortunate both to play with and be taught by him, the latter including hours of "hand-strengthening" via beating huge truck tires with old iron clubs. I never came close enough to his vision of perfect hand action to be relieved of such periodic torture, but, with his help, became good enough not to seriously embarrass myself in a number of national amateur tournaments and championships.

In an appropriate mood, Henry was a marvelous conversationalist, but the one line of his that has stayed most vividly with me involves putting, at which advancing years eventually brought the "Maestro" much misery.

Watching Arnold Palmer struggling on a practice putting green at a British Open long after Arnie's heyday, Sir Henry began talking about how the aging golfer's eyes never accurately "see" the correct line—always an inch or two off to one side or the other, he believed. But then, smiling wryly, he closed the subject with: "But in the end you know, old boy, it's just like sex. One's only got so many shots in one."

thirty-three

TOO DIFFICULT?

With single-round green fees at elite resort or "daily fee" courses approaching $500 as just one example of golf's ever-escalating commercial exploitation, clearly cost is a major factor—perhaps *the* major factor—in the early 21st century's seemingly unstoppable decline of both numbers of players and rounds played.

Most surely, another major contributor to diminishing participation in the game in the U.S. is time. Golf at its American 21st-century pace simply eats up too many of their largely already limited leisure hours for the great majority of citizens.

Then there's a much-less-discussed third dilemma, as expressed most succinctly by 38-time LPGA Tour winner Carol Mann in an interview in *Golf Digest* magazine, and exemplified by the claim of "championship" caliber in every for-profit golf course developer's pitch materials.

"I've seen many surveys asking people why they leave [golf]," Mann said, "and I'm just stunned that the number one reason is never on the questionnaire. Yes, people leave because it's time-consuming. Yes, it's expensive. But the main reason is, it's too difficult. People do not like to do things they are not competent at, period! If we could just own up to that, maybe we could address ways to make the game a little easier, a little more fun, a little easier to excel at, at least at the grassroots level."

Watching the efforts of run-of-the-mill players through traveling so extensively around the game, I've believed the same for years.

So, very well said, Carol.

But is anyone who could do something about that situation listening—and really *hearing*? Judging by the designs of most of the new courses I've played in recent years, I very much doubt it.

part three

CHARACTERS

thirty-four

"LET THE BUGGER GO!"

Exceptional "characters" are few and far between in today's golf-writing gig, as their profession—along with so much of life generally—becomes ever more ritualized and conformist. But that was far from the case in my early days.

I could, for instance, tell many diverting tales about Leonard Crawley, the ultra "establishment" one-time superlative amateur golfer and cricketer (he played for England at both), who reported on golf for a major British newspaper during my early magazine-editing stints. And even more come to mind about his arch-rival, sometimes foe, and at other times bosom friend, the inimitable Henry Longhurst. But we'll limit it here to a few individual remembrances in each case, then one joint interlude.

Crawley first, beginning with our first encounter:

Having driven through the night to cover my first British Amateur, I arrived around dawn at the Royal Liverpool Golf Club at Hoylake to find the clubhouse closed and locked with zero signs of human life. Wandering the premises, eventually I came across a tent that I assumed would be for media use, and, anxious to escape the chill, entered its dark interior through a loose flap. Discovering no temperature improvement, I was about to leave, when a voice out of nowhere boomed, "And *who* are *you?*"

Squinting in its direction, I eventually made out an elderly, tweed-clad, shirt-and-tied, puce-faced, heavily mustachioed, nose-in-the-air figure staring at me with what appeared to be a combination of deep suspicion and considerable disdain over a pair of pince-nez from a seat at a table deep in the tent's recesses.

Suspecting this ogre might be about to go for the cops, I somewhat hesitantly blurted my name and that of the magazine I represented, whereupon he gave a single sharp nod, followed by the statement, "Ah! New fella, eh? Just starting in this ridiculous business. Well, you'll come to regret it, I assure you."

Unable to think of anything else to say to so commanding a figure and intimidating a remark, I got off a simple "Yes, *sir*," while almost standing at attention as he rose and marched over to me.

"Well," he barked, "I'm Crawley. Cover this stuff for the *Telegraph*. Rotten outfit. Never have paid me enough, so I cheat on expenses. Everyone knows, but got away with it for years." Then, peering at me sternly over his nose-perched glasses, he inquired, "Assume you just arrived, what? Well, had any breakfast yet? Only one place open around here at this godforsaken hour. Awful, absolutely awful, but at least it fills a hole." Turning and beginning to walk away, he added, "Come along and join me."

It emerged as an order rather than an invitation, so, of course, I did. And, as ever after on such occasions, the tab simply sat there until I picked it up, and we became friends—well, sort of.

All golf writers (probably all writers) strive hardest with what's known as the "lead"—the opening of whatever they're composing. Working for a "serious" newspaper, Crawley's routinely tended to be pretty mundane, but he did also famously produce surely the most singular opening to a golf report in the game's history.

It happened when, after being upset by his treatment on arrival at a Paris airport, Leonard began his next morning's *Daily Telegraph* report with: "Despite the abominable treatment of the British press by the French customs, the French Open Championship began yesterday on a modest note…"

We all loved him for it.

One of golf writing's great entertainments way back when was secretly watching this redoubtable character, periodically clad in a crimson woolen Churchillian-type "siren-suit" and a huge white Stetson in 90-plus press-facility heat and humidity, his face the color of a fire truck, dictating his Masters Tournament reports in his supremely upper-class English accent to a young freelancing Georgia-born-and-bred stenographer.

A Venusian could have conversed with a Martian more easily!

On now to another of the profession's immortal characters, the aforesaid Longhurst:

To what he regarded as over-fawning admirers of his immensely popular weekly *Sunday Times* column—it usually started off with at least a remark or two about some aspect of golf, but then wandered wherever the great man's mind took him—Henry liked to point out that it's positioning "below the fold" of the paper's back page made it supremely convenient for reading while "doing one's morning business."

The foyer of the Augusta National clubhouse features a small but fully enclosed telephone booth, that, under certain circumstances—an especially heavy intake of gin, for example—could be mistaken for an old-fashioned elevator ("lift" in British). Those present at the time will never forget the Masters evening when Mr. Longhurst was ultimately rescued from said booth after a lengthy interment, while mumbling incoherently something along the lines of, "This damn lift never goes anywhere!"

The 1973 Masters was won by the genial Georgian Tommy Aaron, at which time Longhurst—by then a broadcaster as well as reporter/columnist—was working the telecast for CBS Sports from the 15th-hole tower. It was there that I also happened to have found a shady spot from which to observe what clearly was going to be some extremely critical action.

When, battling for the title with J.C. Snead and Peter Oosterhuis, Aaron made a 14-foot birdie putt off a greenside bunker shot at that hole to take the lead, the gallery roar for the native son was loud and long. Stunningly, however, it appeared to have zero affect on CBS's man, whose only reaction was a slight lift of the hands followed by silent staring at his monitor as cameras panned back and forth over the howling throngs.

Edging closer to the booth entrance as Henry sustained his silence, suddenly I heard the voice of the telecast's equally legendary producer-director, Frank Chirkinian, through the stage-manager's headphones as she lifted one earpiece to avoid being deafened. What Chirkinian—fondly known by his crews as the "Ayatollah"—bellowed was along the lines of, "*Say something, any damn thing, you [blankety-blank] limey!*"

Still motionless and speechless, Longhurst continued solemnly studying his monitor until the uproar had completely quieted. Whereupon he leaned back an inch or two, folded his hands on his ample stomach, smiled slightly, and uttered into his microphone by far the two most memorable words of our long friendship: "Good putt."

Upon discovering late in life that he had contracted inoperable cancer, Henry decided that a "comfortable" suicide was preferable to a drawn-out and inevitably arduous passing. Accordingly, one winter evening, armed with a sufficiency of pills to do the job, he seated himself in his most comfortable chair in front a roaring fire, along with the pills plus a glass and a bottle of his favorite Scotch on a side table.

The plan, of course, was to imbibe sufficient whisky to obviate all pain and distress upon swallowing the pills, then slip away to meet his maker. But there was a hitch. Unfortunately or fortunately, depending on one's take on the man, unconsciousness coincided with his depletion of the Scotch, resulting in him awakening to an empty bottle, an untouched supply of poison pills, and a *humongous* hangover.

And he even had the *savior faire* to make the incident the basis of a column!

One of the last non-family members to visit Henry Longhurst before his eventual demise from the aforesaid cancer was his great friend and TV golf-announcing successor Peter Alliss, who, like his father Percy, had been a top British tournament pro in his younger days. Longhurst's acceptance of and courage regarding his fate was wonderfully expressed in one of his final remarks to Alliss: "Don't worry, old chap. I'll just go on ahead and be sure the hospitality room is all ready for us."

Now to a tale of the twosome:

The occasion was the Walker Cup Match of 1965 at the Baltimore Country Club, more colloquially known as Five Farms.

Having been monstrously, as they say, "over-served" for the better part of a day, Henry early one evening had appointed me his savior and keeper in terms of obtaining a courtesy-car ride for him from the course to the media's downtown hotel. Exacerbating his concern about being stranded overnight in the Maryland boonies was that he had agreed to join Britain's ambassador to the U.S. the next day at his Washington embassy for lunch with a couple of senators, which clearly required a change of clothes, a badly needed cleanup, a huge intake of aspirin, and as much sleep as possible.

Because Leonard Crawley was often late completing and transmitting his reports, and Longhurst was persuaded by some new American friends to continue imbibing long after play ended, it so happened that both men would have to ride in the one courtesy car, the driver of which—a young college student—I'd been able to bribe into doing overtime. His was a splendid machine for the times—a huge Pontiac convertible seemingly straight off the factory floor. With the temperature and humidity still high, the youngster had kept the top of the car down for the greater comfort of his passengers. Crawley took the front seat next to him, and Longhurst somehow managed to stagger and semi-crawl into the back, where I then joined him.

At that point in time it so happened that both men were engaged in one of their fairly regular phases of, if not bitter enmity, at least "not speaking" to each other—a form of hauteur and disdain hanging over from their British upper-class backgrounds. And, in fact, although wordlessly, Crawley had clearly indicated his feelings about Henry's condition via body language, facial expressions, and gestures during Longhurst's lugubrious embarkation process.

The route into the city was partly by freeway. We had been riding on it just long enough for the young driver to gun the car to well over the speed limit—he had informed me as we were setting off that he was late for a *very* important date—when Henry's conscience clicked in. Not for the first time, this precipitated a litany of mumbled, garbled self-abuse about his habitual overindulgence, the certainty of his never being able to get to Washington in time for the ambassador and the senators, and assorted other sins, which suddenly crescendoed with him deciding to end it all there and then.

Turning, he began struggling to ascend the car's rear seat back with, clearly, the objective of positioning himself on its trunk, from where, I assumed, it was his intention, as soon as a sufficiently large truck conveniently positioned itself, to eject himself into its thundering path.

Realizing, as he managed to clamber sufficiently out of the car to spread-eagle much of his torso on the trunk, that he might just be far enough gone to commit such an act, I dived for his legs, grabbed them tightly, and began hauling him—moaning and protesting—back into the seat.

As this episode had begun, Crawley had half-turned to watch it unfold, his expression of disgust and disdain steadily escalating. But it wasn't until I began hauling Henry back into the Pontiac that Leonard decided to intervene.

"Dammit," he roared. "Dammit it all! After all these years, I swear, *enough is enough*. Just let the bugger go, do you hear me? Just *let the bugger go!*"

Periodically in later years—at least during their further "non-speaking" spells—Leonard Crawley would invariably inform me, "I still say you should have done the world a favor and let the bugger go."

Their frequent imbibing together at tournaments indicated, of course, how little he meant it.

thirty-five

STARS:
"PROXIMITY BREEDS
DISENCHANTMENT"

One of history's most polished and prolific writers about golf was an erudite, mercurial, and remarkably energetic—sometimes even frenetic—Englishman called Pat Ward-Thomas. His initial claim to fame—although he never traded on it—was the construction of a rudimentary but, for the inmates, sanity-saving golf course within the grounds of a German prison camp after being shot down during a Royal Air Force World War II mission. Equally remarkably, Pat managed to obtain clubs with the help of the R and A and the Red Cross, then taught himself and his fellow officer prisoners how to create balls out of rubber cushions and shoe leather.

In 1990, eight years after Pat's death, his great friend and America's all-time premier writer about the game, the late Herbert Warren Wind, together with another pal, Robert MacDonald, cofounder and then publisher of the *Classics of Golf* book series, assembled a collection of Ward-Thomas's finest essays for release under that imprint.

Titled "The Lay of the Land," the entire volume to me—also a friend and great admirer of Pat—was not only an immensely informative volume about the great golfers of his lifetime, but, in terms of literacy and judgmental acuity, a small masterpiece.

Here is what has long remained for me one of the most succinct and accurate of its many remarkable passages:

We all have our heroes, and it is the nature of most of the English-speaking races to find them in games players. Often they last beyond the days of adoring youth because the worshipper from afar never really gets to know them. It is well that this should be so, for the gods often have feet of clay; proximity breeds disenchantment.

It can be disconcerting to find that some handsome flannelled idol of the cricket field has the mind of a child; that the artist of the football pitch is unaware and uncaring of the beauty he creates, and is thinking only of his bonus; or that the magnificence of golfers can shrink the moment they leave the green. The writer soon learns, unwillingly perhaps, of the weaknesses of one, the vices of another, and the meanness—that deadly destroyer of hero-worship—of a third. He realizes that most games players are ordinary human beings; they may have become entertaining companions, even friends, but they are no longer heroes, for the magic imagined will have vanished.

Human beings cannot be perfect all the time, although many in the public eye are often unreasonably expected to be so. It is hard therefore to criticize a famous player for having exactly the same faults as other people without their opportunity of concealment. It is difficult to retain a sense of proportion when adulation, in the modern absurdly exaggerated forms, is heaped upon one; it is no small achievement to be normal, balanced, modest, and kind in private when multitudes worship in public. It is exceedingly rare to find a man whose qualities as an individual have never been impaired by his fame as a golfer.

Never, in my view, have truer words been written about sports "stars."

"YOU MISERABLE LITTLE SHITS!"

Following those supremely astute sentiments, a much lighter note about Pat Ainsworth Ward-Thomas, to give him his full name, hopefully is in order.

No one of my golf-writing acquaintance possessed a shorter fuse than he, and especially when covering American major championships and on deadline with his British newspaper report many hours before a day's play ended. That, of course, was occasioned by the five-hour time difference or more between the two countries, meaning he could never give his readers the thing he believed they most wanted—his view on the ultimate chances of whoever was leading.

The outburst under review occurred at the Masters at a time when its "press tent" consisted of an oversized but invariably overpopulated and generally overheated converted Quonset hut, conditions conducive to extreme stress in tight deadline victims that have since been rectified by the creation of, by far, golf's biggest and best-equipped media center.

Jumpy, sweaty, and deeply concerned, as always, about whether the piece was absolutely word perfect, Pat, having completed it, sat back, sighed deeply, and removed his glasses in order to take a much-needed swig of whatever refreshment remained in a paper cup alongside his type-writer (yes, this was long before the days of computerization).

Next, following a glance at his watch and a screeched obscenity on realizing he was considerably late phoning London with the report, he began frantically searching for the glasses without which he would be unable to read it to his faraway copy-taker.

More oaths flew fast and thick as Pat banged about his and his neighbors' table and floor spaces in search of the wretched eyepieces—"Where *are* you, you *miserable* little shits?" was my favorite outburst—until his ire reached a point where he slapped his brow seemingly hard enough to almost K.O. himself.

Whereupon, of course, the spectacles that he'd perched atop his head after typing the last full point and taking refreshment toppled abruptly into his lap, enabling him to grab them up, curse savagely at their predilection for vanishing, then race for the phones, emitting a further obscenity-charged damnation of the world at large and his line of work in particular.

My last memory of the episode as, choking back hysterical laughter, I followed and watched him dial, was, "And you can be sure the f*cking copy-taker will be an absolute cretin—unable to understand a f*cking word of more than one f*cking syllable."

Truly, both a marvelous writer and a world-class curser. But it was best to stand well back when things went awry!

thirty-six

A Literary Genius's Darker Side

Britain's Bernard Darwin (1876–1961), a grandson of the legendary evolutionist Charles Darwin, was and to me remains history's most felicitous golf reporter, essayist, and author. Many of the younger Darwin's peers have tried to ape his approach to a game he frequently appeared to both adore and abominate—sometimes, it seemed, simultaneously—and, even more, the Dickensian grace and sparkle of his literary mastery. None, in my view, have succeeded.

In America, there is pretty much a consensus among golf scribblers that Herbert Warren Wind (1916–2005) came closest, while largely remaining true to his own loquacious mastery of "New World" literacy in committing his encyclopedic knowledge of golf to the printed page. Wind's personality, however, was also vastly gentler than that of his friend and idol. Indeed, the only quirks I identified in our long association were Herb's seeming inability to walk and talk at the same time; his amazingly sweat-free ability to cover the Masters, in blazing Georgian heat, wearing a tweed suit with a dress shirt and decorous necktie; and a seemingly out-of-character love of jazz, about which he once wrote for his alma mater via the *Yale Record*.

Of "Bernardo," as intimates often called him, I have four memories that will never fade. Unfortunately, all reveal his darker side rather than his charm, humor, intelligence, judgment, and the sweetness of nature periodically reflected in his more autobiographical musings.

The 1959 Walker Cup match was played at Muirfield in Scotland, where I had met Darwin for the first time and, as a young pup of a journalist, been suitably both impressed and intimidated. And it was there that my first unforgettable Darwin "moment" occurred as, accompanied by Jack Nicklaus, the great American amateur, Harvie Ward, emerged early one morning from the clubhouse on the way to a practice round. Such a scene, of course, was unremarkable, except for the sweater Ward was wearing—a vividly horizontal-striped number, the likes of which had probably at that time rarely been seen outside Southern California.

After sizing up Ward and this remarkable rainbow garment with a facial expression evolving into a mixture of distaste and disdain, Bernard signaled to the young man as he approached that he wished to speak to him. When both players accordingly stopped, Darwin performed one more slow neck-to-waist examination of Ward, then, in that marvelously plummy voice of his, inquired: "Tell me, young man. Are those your old school colors, or your own unfortunate choice?"

I don't know which Harvie came closest to: laughing or crying.

The Presidents Putter is a tournament played between members of the elite Oxford and Cambridge Golfing Society each January at Rye, a famous old links on England's southeastern coast, often in frost, biting winds, and even layerings of snow. Darwin, by then well into his eighties, had taken up residence locally, and, very much a member of the "Oxbridge" university establishment—he'd won the Putter in 1924—had decided to pay perhaps his favorite golf event a brief visit despite the bitter weather. As protection against it, although wearing shirt, sweater, jacket, cap, and overcoat, he had also wrapped himself from head to toe in a heavy but less than prepossessing blanket.

Coming across this odd-looking but familiar figure surveying the scene not far from the final green, that other titan of British golf writing, the afore-introduced Pat Ward-Thomas, naturally stopped to exchange greetings. Then, knowing the by-then non-traveling Darwin liked to be kept abreast of developments in the game, Pat began enumerating the talents of a young tournament professional of whom he knew the old man would likely have heard but never seen play.

Face scrunched against the icy wind, Darwin patiently listened to the encomium, then, as Pat concluded with the words, "He's a wonderful putter, too," pulled the blanket tighter around himself, gazed thoughtfully off into Rye's famous sand hills, then uttered the following: "Hmmm. Interesting, interesting. But tell me, Pat, is he also a bit of a shit, just like the rest of them?"

As we bid our adieus and walked on, Ward-Thomas, with a sigh, said, "Ah well, no surprise, really. I should have known what his reaction would be the moment I started the story. Not a great lover of today's professional game is old Bernardo."

In keeping with the times of his prime, most of Darwin's golfing and golf-reporting sojourns were made by train, but, as he aged, the automobile played an ever-increasing role in his travels. Never a patient person, one result was a deep loathing of traffic jams.

Stuck with him in a monster of the species on the way to Scotland one time, a friend observed that such irritants were simply "a price of humanity's progress."

"Not at all," responded Bernardo. "They are entirely due, like so many of the other horrors of modern life, to the fatal spread of education."

Although self-admittedly never as fine a player as he would have loved to be, Bernard Darwin was good enough to have become a semifinalist in the British Amateur and played for his country in the Walker Cup. He also greatly enjoyed and sometimes excelled at alternate-shot foursomes, to the point of once winning Britain's primary tournament of that type partnered by the legendary Joyce Wethered, later Lady Heathcoat-Amory.

Whatever he lacked in the way of ball-striking skills, Darwin was renowned for making up for via extreme competitive intensity, sometimes turning to seething outright fury when things went seriously askew.

Hence his response to another friend who'd just joined a foursomes match in which he and a badly off-form partner were falling irretrievably behind.

"Well, Bernard, old chap, how are you doing?" asked the chum cheerily, as Darwin and his sad-looking partner strode towards a clump of trees into which the latter had just sliced a brassie shot.

Darwin stopped, glared at the slumped shoulders of the man as he kept on walking, considered for a long moment, then—loud enough for the slicer to hear—let fly with the following: "My friend, I would have you know—and the rest of the world, too, if I could think of a way—that *I am tied to a turd*."

Not knowing exactly how you stood with golf's greatest writer was truly a rarity!

thirty-seven

WORKING WITH
MR. ROBERTS

The call came out of the blue from the editorial director of Doubleday, the publishing goliath.

Clifford Roberts, the Augusta National and Masters cofounder with Bob Jones, was writing a book about the two and required help. Was I interested in supplying it? No joint credit, but the pay would be "decent."

You betcha.

Along with his simply appurtenanced room at the quietest end of the ground floor of the Augusta National clubhouse, Mr. Roberts's spartan office in the then-tournament headquarters building was the only interior space on the premises bereft of air-conditioning. Sweating heavily within a few minutes of joining him for our first meeting on the project, I inquired as to why the room was so hot.

Mr. Roberts routinely spoke slowly, sparingly, and monotonically, with many utterances prefaced by an "Ahaar"-type throat-clearing sound.

"Ahaar…because I'm always cold," Mr. Roberts responded, regarding me as though the inquiry was idiotic.

As our previous path-crossings had been cursory at best, my next question was why he'd chosen me as his collaborator. Lying on his credenza—next to the straw hat he always silently lifted and donned when he decided it was time for lunch, or that we'd finished work for the day—was a copy of the book *Golf My Way*, on which I'd collaborated with Jack Nicklaus. Mr. Roberts's reply was simply to slowly turn in his highly uncomfortable-looking chair, silently tap its cover, and nod once.

Mr. Roberts wanted to call his book *The History of the Augusta National Golf Club,* and he kept a note with that title in a desk drawer (the plain and relatively small desk's surface was always empty). At some point I suggested changing "History" to "Story."

"Ahaar...why?" Mr. Roberts inquired.

"Less academic-sounding," I replied. "Should sell more copies."

Silently but with a nod, Mr. Roberts withdrew the note, meticulously crossed out the word "History," then slowly wrote above it "Story."

It may have been my biggest contribution.

Because Mr. Roberts drafted the book himself—and exceptionally well for a nonprofessional writer—my role was simply to advise on section and chapter organization, plus the possible polishing of grammar and syntax. Most of that we did at Augusta National or at one of Mr. Roberts's homes in the mountains of North Carolina. But Mr. Roberts—by then in his early eighties, an insomniac, and increasingly struggling with major health problems—had decided he might die before the thing was completed, so figured a certain urgency was—to use one of his favorite phrases—"in order."

I never counted the number of times our bedroom phone—which was on my wife's night stand—rang between midnight and 2:00 in the morning during the months we worked together, but it was at least a dozen.

"Guess who," Jean would mumble as I drowsily accepted the phone.

"Ahaar...Cliff here. You weren't sleeping, were you? Now, about that semicolon on page 184. Ahaar...well, I think it should be a comma, or maybe a hyphen. Think about it, will you? Goodnight."

Could that and all the other items he woke us with have waited until the next morning? In his scheme of things, no way!

Mr. Roberts's habits and preferences were so well known by the Augusta National grill room staff that he seemed never to need to order anything—for lunch, a chicken sandwich followed by one of the club's "signature" peach cobblers arrived automatically. On one occasion—assuming, I guess, that, being with the boss, I couldn't possibly have the *cojones* to choose anything else—the waiter brought me the same sandwich. When I demurred, Mr. Roberts gazed at me stonily for a few seconds, then crooked a finger at a senior club member at a nearby table, and said, after the man trotted over, "Ahaar…Joe, I hear the Masters coincides with Easter a couple of years from now. That won't do, so I need to know who's in charge of scheduling Easter. Find out, will you."

Pondering how he intended to go about getting the date of Easter changed, I forced down the chicken sandwich undemurringly—and, of course, the delicious peach cobbler that followed.

One day, coming out of the club's pro shop, Mr. Roberts and I ran across an extremely successful senior amateur and accomplished businessman who'd just completed a round as the guest of a major corporate-titan member. The senior, a longtime friend, had previously confided to me how desperately and for how long he'd desired to be invited to join the Augusta National, but that it had never happened; and that, of course, he daren't ask because doing so absolutely guaranteed non-invitation (with the sole exception many years later, word has it, of Bill Gates—by which time Mr. Roberts was dead). But at that moment our senior champ apparently just couldn't stop himself from very diplomatically voicing his life's greatest ambition to Mr. Roberts.

There came the usual silently grim stare, followed by the "Ahaar," then this brief response: "[Name of supplicant], the fact is, we already have a member from [name of supplicant's home town]."

From the look on my pal's face, it's a miracle he didn't instantly crumple into a writhing heap.

During our work time at the Augusta National, each day precisely at 5:00 PM Mr. Roberts's right arm snaked slowly behind him, to lift and place squarely on his head that famous straw hat—often when I was in the middle of making what I considered a critical grammatical or syntactical point. Whereupon the two of us set out on a slow walk, one evening on the course's front nine, the next on the back. Completing one such saunter, I mentioned how healthy and fresh the hanging-basket flowers lining the clubhouse's roofed frontal walkway looked.

"Ahaar…and so they should," came the growl.

"Why?" I asked, more for want of something to say than from curiosity.

"Ahaar…because they're made of plastic."

Plastic flowers at the Augusta National! I couldn't believe it. "But why?" I asked again, the shock surely clear in my tone.

"Ahaar...so they don't drop petals and crap all over the carpeting," came the answer.

But still my most vivid memory of our association was the look on Jack Nicklaus's face at Mr. Roberts's response to a suggestion the Golden Bear voiced as the three of us lunched in the grill room one day.

As mentioned earlier, by then a pattern had been established of me accompanying Jack to Augusta National the week before the Masters so we could meet after dinner each evening to tape-record for articles and books we were collaborating on—this, of course, following his daytime practice sessions and rounds of the course.

Apparently feeling like company for his planned afternoon 18, Nicklaus suddenly said, "Kenny, you're at loose ends until this evening, right? So how about playing with me?"

Quickly for him, Mr. Roberts's eyes had risen from his plate to Jack's as he made the suggestion. Whereupon the Bear—having noted the move and spotted something in the old man's expression—quickly added, "No problem for you in that, right, Cliff?"

Slowly now, Mr. Roberts lowered the piece of (chicken) sandwich he was about to bite into back to his plate.

"Ahaar...Jack, that'll be just fine if we can get a member to join the two of you."

It was the only time I've seen Jack Nicklaus dumbstruck. By then he'd won five Masters, and—although only later elected to full membership of the club—was clearly under the impression that courtesies afforded to winners of green jackets, the legendary badge of "belonging," included inviting and playing with guests.

But not so, explained Mr. Roberts: the Augusta National rule was that a *bona fide* member must always—repeat, *always*—accompany any and every guest. Whereupon he signaled the head waiter to fetch the club's manager, spoke quietly with him for a moment, then turned back to Jack.

"Fortunately, we have a local member whom I am sure will oblige. He's a bit long in the tooth, so he'll play from the forward tees, but you'll find him a fine gentleman. He'll be here by the time you change your shoes." Then, switching that stony old gaze to me, he concluded, "Ahaar…so go ahead and enjoy your round."

Later, I heard the same thing had happened to four-time Masters champion Arnold Palmer when he wanted to play the Augusta National with his father one time.

There's also the story of Mr. Roberts's remarks to a nonmember U.S. senator who somehow got to play the course with another non-belonger: "Mr. Senator, it is in the Augusta National Golf Club's bylaws that guests must play with a member. Well, now that you've played, don't bother coming back."

Or, in short, at America's most famous and elite club—at least in Mr. Roberts's day—the rules were the rules were the rules.

With absolutely no exceptions.

thirty-eight

"LIKE STALIN RULED RUSSIA"

Although the great amateur Bob Jones, who became president in perpetuity, birthed the concept of the Augusta National Golf Club, it was Clifford Roberts who made it happen.

As the first chairman, Roberts found the land for the club; arranged its purchase; supervised down to the finest detail every element of the creative work; saved the place from bankruptcy in its many Great Depression downers; originated most of and supervised all of the course's never-ending "improvements" (his word) over its first four-plus decades; saw the club and tournament through endless civil-rights brouhahas and a world war; and endlessly upgraded and refined what became the Masters (out of modesty, Jones had originally insisted on calling it the Augusta National Invitation Tournament). Or, as a member who was clearly scared to death of him once put it to me, "He ran the whole thing like Stalin ruled Russia."

Among Mr. Roberts's best-known power-plays was keeping CBS's rights fees to Masters telecasts considerably lower than what other networks would have paid, and signing only year-to-year contracts with the broadcaster. When I asked him why on both counts, the response was, "Ahaar...so we can tell 'em how to do it."

Mr. Roberts was also responsible for the least amount of TV commercial time in big-time American sports broadcasting (four minutes per hour as opposed to a norm of around 12); and, each year, he reviewed tapes of the Masters coverage, focusing minutely on both the pictorial and verbal elements, then writing letters to the CBS brass, nitpicking the production and announcing efforts and listing dos and don'ts for following years.

He also was adept at convincing major suppliers, such as Coca-Cola, that becoming telecast sponsors, and otherwise assisting the club and tournament financially, was the best way to protect their Masters franchise—sometimes via simply a brief phone call to the company's chairman.

Strolling the back nine with Mr. Roberts one evening, I remembered hearing that the Masters, unlike any other golf tournament I knew about—and despite the fact that just about every able-bodied golfer on the planet would have served there for free—paid all of its volunteers. When I asked why, there came the usual pause, followed by, "Ahaar...so we can fire 'em." (Knowing the man as well as I did by then, I should have known that answer, of course.)

Indeed, so obsessive and autocratic was his control, in even the most minor of matters, that the sick joke circulating around the local newspaper's offices following his suicide was that he "controlled everything down to the last shot."

Despite his wealth, power, and elite business and political associations, the Mr. Roberts I got to know was a singularly plain and frugal man, who would on rare occasions reveal a bone-dry but invariably po-faced sense of humor. His conservatism in all things—political beliefs, lifestyle, bare-bones articulation, intensity of reserve, secretive habits—was total and inviolable. Apart from his invariably green-jacketed garb during his many months of living at the club each year, he is said to have always worn blue suits with identical red ties, of which reputedly he owned a couple dozen. Former USGA executive director Frank Hannigan once described his looks and demeanor as "button-faced and somber—American Gothic."

Some people—especially in the print media—claimed that Mr. Roberts was an out-and-out racist, although I discovered on my visits with him at the Augusta National that many of its more menially employed staff—virtually all of them black—spoke well of his fairness and concern for their welfare. Other staff members praised his generosity to longtime employees experiencing difficulties, and particularly to the wife of one of the club's pros when she contracted a life-threatening illness. But there was also criticism of his stoniness, stubbornness, perfectionism, and ultra-obsessiveness.

Surely many of his characteristics, praiseworthy and otherwise, derived from his background.

Born in the hamlet of Morning Sun, Iowa, on March 6, 1894, Mr. Roberts was the second child of five of Charles DeClifford Roberts Sr., a perpetually financially hard-pressed farmer/real-estate salesman in various parts of the Midwest, and Rebecca Scott Key Roberts, a distant cousin of Francis Scott Key. His ailing mother killed herself with a shotgun at age 44, and his father died at age 50 after being struck by a train, which some believed he had stepped in front of deliberately.

After an altercation with his principal, young Clifford barely made it through high school and never attended college. From the age of 19, he worked as a traveling men's suit salesman, served in the Army, then stumbled into the oil-lease business in Texas, where, at the age of 27, some speculations earned him a substantial sum. With that windfall, he bought a partnership in the Wall Street brokerage then known as Reynolds & Company (later to become Dean Witter Reynolds and presently a part of Morgan Stanley). There—not least through his persistent cultivation of relationships with Bob Jones and many of Jones's pals—Roberts became successful to the point of becoming known, somewhat scathingly, as the "Boy Wonder of Wall Street." Whatever his methods, it was his market success that enabled him financially to increasingly devote the greater part of his time and energy to the Augusta National and the Masters. Although married three times, he fathered no children.

As the years passed, most of any time and energy left over from running the club and the tournament was spent as an intimate of and personal financial and campaign financial advisor to the most famous of Augusta National's ever more elite membership, President Eisenhower. Discovering Ike's passion for the game, Mr. Roberts invited him to visit the club and, after Ike joined in 1948, played frequently with him on his numerous visits. When asked about the great man's shot-making ability, Mr. Roberts drily described him to me as, "Ahaar...a golf nut of the first order who might have given up the presidency if he'd believed that would have made him a better player."

Perhaps the most famous Eisenhower-Roberts anecdote concerns what, although now much farther from the tee than in their day, remains known as "Ike's Tree," a tall loblolly pine in the left-center of the 17th fairway that the president hit so many times he proposed, at a club governors' meeting, that it be removed. Mr. Roberts immediately ruled him out of order and adjourned the meeting.

But nothing better exemplifies the closeness of their relationship than this comment to the leader of the free world after Ike blundered badly in a bridge game one evening at the club: "Mr. President, that's why I can't let you run the country by yourself."

thirty-nine

ULTIMATE DEVOTION

The next time you enjoy watching top pros compete, tip your hat to the man most responsible for player- and spectator-pleasing amenities in the entire history of tournament golf.

Throughout most of his years as Augusta National and Masters czar, Clifford Roberts annually set up committees to recommend changes, improvements, and innovations, the members of which were required to report back to him, *in writing*, following each year's tournament.

But many of the best and ultimately most widely copied ideas worldwide by tournament organizers seemingly were his alone, including:

- Tee-to-green gallery ropes, of which the late, great Byron Nelson liked to tell this story: "I was out on the course with Cliff when he first had that done, and the ropes were all white. He looked around and said, 'White doesn't go in this place at all. The ropes should be green.' And, a couple of days later, by the time that Masters started, they all were green." And have been ever since — along with virtually all the rest of the course's furnishings and appurtenances.

- What you and I would call grandstands or bleachers, but which the club's literature in Roberts's day (and language) referred to as "temporary spectator Observation Stands at locations where several scenes of action may be observed." Or, in other words, precision, precision, precision

- The over/under par system now employed almost universally on golf leader boards to designate players' standings, with black or green numerals for par-and-above totals and red for below par. Leader boards, by the way — and can't you just see Mr. Roberts penning such words!—were referred to in Masters literature during his time as "score reporting services at numerous points on the course."

- Complimentary pairings sheets for all "patrons" (Mr. Roberts's word for spectators or fans).

Nowadays, the Augusta National public relations staff annually puts out a beautifully produced inch-thick, magazine-page-size *Masters Media Guide*, replete with just about every fact and statistic regarding the tournament that could possibly be dug up. Under the heading "Significant Dates," I counted in my latest edition some 35 more Masters additions or innovations conceived and/or implemented during the Roberts's reign (1932–1976), primarily designed to increase "patron" enjoyment of the event. How many were his alone is unclear, but my guess would be the majority.

Elsewhere in that media guide, one further discovers that, during his long reign, Mr. Roberts also mandated or masterminded—usually both—so many golf course "improvements," both major and minor, that the Masters test remained unchanged from one year to the next only a handful of times.

Surely, never has a golf club and event, or possibly any other sports enterprise, enjoyed and benefited from such passionate—if often persnickety—devotion.

forty

MR. ROBERTS
SIGNS OFF

In the late afternoon of September 28, 1977, not long after his book was published, Mr. Roberts asked the Augusta National's in-house barber, Johnny Johnson, to come to his cabin and give him a haircut. Following that, Roberts called his third wife, Betty, an Englishwoman with no love for golf, her husband's club, or his lifestyle, and asked her to come to Augusta as quickly as possible. Living in Beverly Hills, California, she told him she couldn't do so immediately because she needed time to arrange for closing her house.

That night, the Georgia skies were partly cloudy and, although the temperature was in the sixties, the atmosphere a little muggy. After tidying up his room a bit and writing a note, Mr. Roberts slipped a pair of trousers and a trench coat over his pajamas, stepped barefooted into a pair of galoshes, then pocketed a Smith & Wesson .38, the functionality of which he'd previously checked out with a club security guard on the pretext that he'd been hearing night noises around his cabin.

So clad and armed, around 2:30 AM Mr. Roberts slowly began to make his way down the hill to his beloved Ike's Pond, the centerpiece of the club's gorgeous par-3 course. Well into his eighties, weary and unsteady following a recent stroke, and afflicted with incurable cancer, the short walk is believed to have taken him almost half an hour.

On arriving at the pond, he pulled the .38 from his pocket and shot himself dead with a bullet to the head. Crumpled in a creek bed, his body was discovered at 8:00 the next morning. As mentioned, his mother had committed suicide, and also possibly his father.

As Steve Eubanks wrote in his fine book *Augusta, Home of the Masters Tournament*, about Mr. Roberts's choice of location: "This area was safe, away from the main course where spectators would have undoubtedly discovered the spot and created some kind of macabre landmark. This was also most helpful to the staff. Emergency vehicles could access the pond with ease, investigators wouldn't disturb any of the high traffic areas around the clubhouse or the golf course, and it would be an easy spot to clean up."

As he'd requested, Mr. Roberts's body was cremated and his ashes buried in a generally unknown location on the Augusta National property. There was no religious service, ceremony, nor even flowers.

Some time following Mr. Roberts's suicide, a friend of us both showed me a copy of some paperwork he had left behind.

The note to his then-wife said simply, "Sorry, Betty. Love, Cliff." Attached to it were copies of hospital reports concerning the deadly seriousness of the ailments from which he was suffering, and that his doctors had told him could only become worse.

I asked the friend who showed me the papers why he thought Mr. Roberts had killed himself.

He replied, "The primary reason, I suspect, was that he just could not live with the prospect of being even the tiniest bit out of control of himself."

forty-one

CHARACTERS OR JACKASSES?

As some traveling American golfers surely have experienced, certain golf club "secretaries" (general managers in the U.S.) at the supposedly "better" British clubs are inclined, by nature or choice, to go about their business in a manner ranging from stuffy to flat-out snooty. Visitors whom they deem possessed of inferior nationality, occupation, schooling, appearance, or speaking accents usually suffer the worst nose-in-the-air treatment.

In years gone by, much of this snobbishness derived from so many of these officials being retired army, air force, or naval officers, whose service had infected them with a sense of superiority to anyone known or assumed to be of lesser rank. A sure sign of the disease was—and in some cases still is—use of their military titles in all forms of printed matter related to their club's affairs, and even conversationally, especially when addressing the lower orders.

By far the most infamous of these "characters" was a now long-deceased former naval captain by the name of P.W.T. "Paddy" Hanmer, secretary from 1968 to 1983 of the Honourable Company of Edinburgh Golfers at Muirfield in Scotland, a club that surely strives harder than any other in the U.K. to sustain a reputation for elitism. As thousands of the man's victims still burn upon remembering, Hanmer's greatest joy in life appeared to be behaving like a jackass to visiting Americans—including, perhaps most famously, one who had just won his third of an eventual five Open Championship over the famous links.

It happened like this.

Late on the Sunday evening following that victory in 1980, Tom Watson, inspired by pal Ben Crenshaw, with their wives and a couple of other players and some pals in tow—just possibly following a celebratory intake of what normal Scots call "wee drams"—slipped onto the empty course with an assortment of antique hickory-shafted clubs and gutta percha balls conjured out of who knows where by dedicated golf historian and collector Crenshaw. Ben's proposal was that they "play a few holes the way they used to be played."

Amid a good deal of joviality, the group had played up the 10th hole and was on its way down 18 in semi-darkness when a puce-faced, pear-shaped man burst out of the clubhouse and came streaking down the fairway, flashlight bobbing furiously on the gang of evildoers. Arriving within earshot, he bellowed, among other things, "This is no *playground!*" and "I'll see to it that all of you are banned from this course *forever!*"

Their threatener was, of course, the inimitable Hanmer, seemingly enraged to the point of having the entire group walk the plank, had such been possible so far from the course's abutting Firth of Forth.

Another example of Hanmer's "style" was summarily ejecting from the premises the president of *Golf Digest* magazine and the publisher of *Sports Illustrated*, along with two friends, after they joined up as a fourball on the totally empty Muirfield course, following his insistence that they start as "singles" due to the "busyness" of the place. Hanmer had discovered the offense via binoculars kept in his office for identifying just such atrocities, and sped out to the group on another disciplinary tool, a noisy and odorous moped.

Hanmer was known to have flatly rejected requests from at least two U.S. multiple major champions, among many other golfing notables, for tee times. But his greatest fame drew from telling lesser supplicants—and especially Yanks who simply showed up on the off chance—after sweeping the virtually empty fairways with the aforementioned binoculars— "Sorry, but the course is far too busy to accommodate you today."

That he survived so long in so powerful a position was due primarily to the majority of the club's membership, drawn from the upper crust of Edinburgh society, regarding him as a marvelous "character" and his appalling manners as hilarious. Typical of their mentality was the popularity of the supposedly jocular line, "Welcome to Muirfield—Please leave at once."

In the absence of official handicaps, Muirfield members negotiate either over generally well-lubricated clubhouse meals or on the 1st tee the number of shots to be given or taken in their most popular match, the fast-moving "foursome," in which teams of two hit alternately. An all-male establishment, the club's misogyny at one point was such that keeping women off the premises entirely was virtually a mandate. Indeed, so strictly was this policy pursued that, years ago, while the club's kitchens were being renovated, members ate at the adjoining comparably haughty Greywalls Hotel, which, gladly abiding by its neighbor's tradition, refused to seat women for that meal.

Hanmer's immediate successor—another ex-military type—could be even more offensive, once bursting from his office during a British Open to order a group containing four of the world's top players, socializing by the clubhouse front entrance, to "Take your coffee-klatching somewhere else." The latest incumbent reputedly is no pushover either with unwanted visitors, but apparently no one now leaves feeling flat-out insulted.

The Muirfield course is, beyond question, a magnificent test of the game—in fact, perhaps the best-designed and conditioned, not to mention the fairest, of all Britain's major links layouts. And so, of course, thousands want to play there.

The good news in that regard is that reportedly there are now opportunities in many weeks to play either on a Tuesday or a Thursday, for some 100-plus visitors, both men and women, given they possess certified handicaps no higher respectively than 18 or 24.

The irritating news is that everyone must enter the clubhouse "well-dressed" (meaning for men primarily jacket and tie), change into golf attire to play, then change back into the original outfit to eat in or otherwise use the clubhouse facilities following a round—a requirement that gave rise to the old joke that clothes are on and off more at the Hon. Co. than in a brothel!

The really bad news, an Edinburgh writer friend recently told me, is that demand still vastly exceeds supply. He added that either an introduction by a member or an early and formal approach—meaning by letter, with credentials specified—offers the best chance.

And finally, he warns, the green fee "ain't exactly peanuts."

A DISQUALIFYING FACTOR

The foregoing brings to mind a joke recently heard from a British secretary who never served in the armed forces, never wears an old-school tie, doesn't drink "pink gins," and tends to call everyone by their first names immediately upon meeting them.

Seems the "Hon Sec" at a top club had finally drunk himself to death, whereupon a selection committee was formed to interview replacements.

The first inquisition went well until the end, when the club's oldest member, a celebrated lord of the realm, suddenly asked the candidate a stunning question: "I regret having to raise this delicate matter, my good man, but have you by any chance been, well…circumcised?"

The candidate harrumphed, blushed, shuffled around uncomfortably in his chair for a long moment, then finally plucked up the courage to respond. "Frankly, sir, I am stunned that a person of your eminence would even dream of asking such a question, and, even at the risk of jeopardizing my chance at this much-desired position, I must insist on knowing why."

"Well," responded Lord Whatsisname, "as you know, we are one of the oldest and most distinguished clubs in this country, which means that we have always had a complete prick for a secretary. So I am afraid that circumcision is a disqualifying factor."

FUNNY OR SAD?

Finally, regarding British golf and just for fun, here's a famous joke—over there, at least—reflecting surely the ultimate poke at that nation's one-time degree of golfing elitism:

Into the parking lot of let's call it the Royal Nameless G.C. rolls a gorgeous vintage Bentley, from which emerges a distinguished looking man dressed as everyone once did for golf in the top echelons of the game in the U.K.—elegant plus-four suit, expensive highly polished brogues, loudly checkered dress shirt, and colorfully striped tie denoting the man's membership in an almost equally upscale club.

Striding into the golf shop, he sees the pro standing behind the counter, walks over, and addresses him in a commanding upper-class bray.

"I say, my man, I've always wanted to play here, was passing by with time on my hands, and wondered if I might enjoy a quick round? Happy to pay whatever the green is, of course."

The pro's expression becomes one of embarassment.

"Sir, I'm afraid that, this being an extremely exclusive club, as I'm sure you know, I do not have the authority to permit you on the course. However, I will be glad to introduce you to our secretary, who is the only person who can authorize your playing."

"Righto, old chap," responds the visitor, and off they go the secretary's office, where the pro meekly explains the purpose of the visit.

Outfitted almost identically to the supplicant, the secretary leans back in his CEO-style swivel chair and silently looks the visitor up and down a number of times. Finally, he says, "As you might expect of all, er, walk-ins, short of an introduction from a member, permision to play here is dependent on a person's credentials. So I must ask you some personal questions."

The walk-in's eyebrows have shot up, but after a few seconds he nods agreement.

Reading spectacles pushed to the end of his nose in order to get a better look at the intruder, the secretary begins the inquisition.

"Residence?"

"Mayfair and Pebble Beach," responds his victim crisply.

"School?"

"Eton."

"University?"

"Cambridge. First-class honors graduate."

The secretary: "I assume you served in the war. Regiment?"

"Guards. Awarded the Victoria Cross following D-Day."

"Rank?"

"On leaving the service, major-general."

The secretary folds his hands in his lap and ponders silently for a few moments, then looks up at the pro.

"Very well," he says. "Nine holes."

With which he returns to his paperwork.

forty-two

OO7

Sean Connery was one of numerous showbiz giants I got to know through years of coproducing pro-celebrity TV golf shows with the BBC (*see page 156*), and with whom, over time, our mutual passion for the game cemented a close friendship.

Although not as consistent a shot-maker as he would have liked to be, OO7's competitiveness—as intense as I've encountered outside of top tournament play—made him a tough adversary, and especially when a sizable wager was at stake, as was invariably the case in any game in which he participated. Win a few quid or bucks off Sir Sean (he was knighted some years ago), and you knew you'd played at or very close to your best.

The combination of Connery's friendship with Jack Nicklaus and myself, plus the amount of time he spent filming in the States, where he had a Los Angeles home, eventually led to him adding Muirfield Village to his numerous American club memberships, and becoming a regular participant in the Memorial Tournament's early years pro-ams.

Through those visits, he also discovered one of golf's best-kept secrets outside of Ohio, which is that few cities of comparable size possess as many outstanding golf courses as that state's capital of Columbus. Accordingly, when I suggested to him that we spend a few days playing the best of them outside of Memorial week, he leapt at the idea.

Our base would be Muirfield Village, where we'd stay in one of its comfortable villas, set in a pleasantly wooded area adjacent to the opening hole. Each of them at that time had five bedrooms, but, in respect to OO7's eminence, I insisted he take the master suite.

That first night we enjoyed an early dinner and chatted a while on the villa's deck, before retiring to our respective rooms fairly early to be ready for a possible 36 holes the next day at Scioto, the famed club near where Nicklaus grew up and learned the game.

Deeply asleep, I never really registered the time, but I guess it was around 3:00 AM when all hell broke across the hall in the master suite—sudden yelling and banging noises growing rapidly louder and louder.

Concerned that some bad guys had discovered the presence of a star and were trying either to rob him or checking whether "James Bond" was as tough as his movies suggested, I leapt out of bed, rushed across the hall, and shoved open the door.

And what a sight I beheld!

Sean, as he explained later, had turned off the air-conditioning but, being a fresh-air addict, opened the sliding windows onto his portion of the deck.

All had then remained normal until, as he lay dreaming of breaking par at Scioto, he discovered he had an intruder when whatever it was made a noise by knocking something over. Switching on his bedside lamp, he discovered an exceptionally large raccoon giving him the evil eye from what seemed like an attack-ready crouch at the bottom of his king-size bed.

Both of us had taken our golf clubs into our rooms in readiness for our early start. Figuring they were the only weapons available, Sean had leapt out of bed, hauled a wedge from his bag, jumped back up on the king-size, and now—clad only in boxers and T-shirt—appeared to be challenging his visitor to a sword fight while bellowing a mixture of threats and Scottish invective at the now petrified creature.

It was unfair, of course, but—having, like the rest of humanity, been so impressed by all of that Bondian dash and suavity in all of those movies—all I could do was laugh hysterically.

As I did so, the visitor, seeing and hearing the wedge's head whistle closer and closer to its own, suddenly had the good sense to leap off the bed, scamper across the room, and disappear whence it came.

I continued to laugh until, noting the club still in my friend's hand—along with the, shall we just say, distinctly grim expression on his face—I quickly slipped from the room, hustled to mine, and locked the door behind me.

As I'd learned on the golf course, it did not do to remain in the immediate presence of an extremely angry 007.

Cut to another time in Ohio, with Connery and I off very early to play The Country Club, then rush for flights home.

We overnighted at Muirfield Village again, but, with no Monday food service there, drove around the local then-village (now sizeable town) of Dublin looking for a decent breakfast spot, only to discover the only place open was a McDonald's. As I pulled into its parking lot, Connery said, "You have to be *kidding*," but we were both hungry, so what the heck.

He stepped inside first, looked around, approached the service counter, and began studying the placarded menu.

The five female staffers present glanced at him casually as we entered, then stared disbelievingly as he approached the counter. Finally deciding that what surely must be an apparition had appeared before them, they became frozen in place, mute, did double takes, clearly all of them way beyond believing what they were seeing. Finally, the one closest to me whispered, "Is *he* who we think *he* is?"

I nodded, whereupon she turned to her coworkers and did the same. There were gasps, twitterings, even more wide-eyed stares, with the oldest of the ladies looking like she might faint.

Connery completed his menu review, then raised an eyebrow to the blushing girl who had summoned the nerve to approach to within a few yards of the great man to hesitantly ask what he would like to eat.

In that gorgeous Scottish baritone, 007 intoned politely, "I canna see anything up there I particularly care for, my dear. But, tell me, would you happen to have any soft-boiled eggs?"

All mouths dropped, stunned silence reigned, until finally the brave little waitress slowly shook her head.

James Bond harrumped, shrugged, turned, and exited. Following, I heard him mumbling to himself about how any restaurant could possibly fail to be able to meet so simple and routine a breakfast order as soft-boiled eggs.

I bet some of those ladies still think it never really happened.

forty-three

SCOTTISH LOOPERS

After playing golf in many countries, frequently with caddies, I am convinced that Scots loopers are by far the most outspoken of the breed—or perhaps the word should be *candid*.

Here are a few of the comebacks I've either received or overhead from professional caddies on Scottish links, and especially at the more elite clubs where the veterans seem to proliferate. All the victims—myself included—were playing somewhere between poorly and terribly at the time of the interchange.

Golfer: "Oh my, it's a funny old game, isn't it?"
Caddie: "Aye, sir, 'tis that for some. But it's nay meant to be."

Golfer: "See this creek? Well, I hate this game so much I think I'm gonna drown myself in it."
Caddie: "Ah, weel, that'll be just foine, sir. But are ye sure ye can keep ye're head still long enough?"

Golfer: "I'd move heaven and earth to break 100 on this great course."
Caddie: "Weel, I suggest ye try heaven, sir. Because ye've already moved most of Earth."

Golfer: "Can I get there with the 5 iron?"
Caddie: "Eventually, sir. Eventually."

Golfer: "Please stop distracting me by constantly checking your watch."
Caddie: "It's nay a watch, sir. It's a compass."

Golfer: "Well, old fellow, what do you think of my game after the first nine?"

Caddie: "I hope ye won't mind ma saying it, but I prefer golf, sir."

Golfer: "Damn it, this may be the worst course I ever played."

Caddie: "Bain't the course, sir. We left that quite a while ago."

Golfer (addressing fellow-customer in Carnoustie-adoining bar prior to playing the course): "The owner tells me you caddie here. How's the course playing?"

Caddie: "The course is playing just foine, sir—that being ye have a game."

Most of my experiences with Scots caddies have been both enjoyable and helpful. But two didn't quite fit that description.

Scene one. I'm playing Royal Troon, and, in the standard American manner, on the first four holes I ask my caddie the distances in yards of my approach shots. The old fellow's response is to withdraw a club from my bag and hand it to me with a silent nod of his head. Although hitting decent shots, with this procedure I am alternately over the first green, short of the second, over the third, then short again.

Number 5 is a par 3, but the tee markers are set some distance from a yardage marker, so once again I ask for a yardage. Yet again, a club is withdrawn from the bag and proffered with a silent nod of the head.

But by then I've more than had enough.

"No, Jimmy," I tell my man, thrusting the club back in the bag, "not this time. *This* time, I want to know the *exact* distance from the tee markers to the pin in yards before *I* decide what to hit."

Whereupon the old geezer eyes me balefully, spits forcibly, wrenches the bag from his shoulder, tosses it into some deep grass, and growls, "If ye'll nay play as I club ye, I'll nay carry your fooking clubs." With which he disappears in the direction of the clubhouse as fast as his bandy little legs will carry him.

Scene two. My wife and I are playing the Queen's course at Gleneagles late on a beautiful summer afternoon. I'm carrying a light bag but, with a heavier one, Jean prefers a looper and expresses that wish to the caddie master.

"Weel, noo, ma'am," says the good man, "we're awfully busy and"—pointing to a down-at-heel ancient supporting a nearby wall—"I'm afraid the only one left is old Billy over there. He's a braw man in many ways, and a foine, foine caddie, but...weel, to tell ye the truth, zur, he's been 'refreshing' himself just a wee bit since his morning round, so..."

He shrugged and left the rest to our imagination.

Despite my misgivings as to the meaning of "refreshing himself," we decide to hire the old boy, and—beyond him briefly disappearing behind trees or bushes every couple of holes as he trails arthritically behind us—all goes well until we arrive at a highly elevated tee early on the back nine, where our puce faced, hard-breathing, heavily sweating Billy boy clearly has an awful struggle climbing the slope.

Finally he makes it, and I hit, after which we walk forward to the women's tee. There, when my wife about-faces to take a club from Billy, both he and her bag have totally vanished, as though suddenly spirited from the face of the planet by some heavenly power.

Surprised, puzzled, and concerned, we begin a rapid inspection of the surrounding terrain. And, lo and behold, within a few seconds we spot an apparently unconscious Billy partially immersed in a small pond 20 or so feet below us at the base of the tee, with the weight of his now saturated heavy woolen overcoat lowering him ever deeper into the water. Scrambling down the bank and into the shallows, we each grab an arm and haul the old boy to dry land just before his head goes under. Whereupon, with his overcoat suddenly flopping open as he rolls over, a rather fancy brown bottle slips from its inside pocket.

Retrieving it, three things strike me: First, in the course of "refreshing" himself Jimmy has completely emptied the bottle. Second, its label indicates that it once contained an exceptionally fine brand of single-malt Scotch whisky. Third, the costliness of the brand suggested that whoever had hired our man that morning had definitely overpaid him.

By now semiconscious, Billy sinks his head to the grass for a much-needed snooze as he weakly waves us on our way.

Meaning, of course, I get to carry both sets of clubs.

forty-four

CHURCHILL ON GOLF

In his spare time Sir Winston Churchill painted and built brick walls but was never a golfer. However, he apparently once tried the game when on vacation while still serving in Britain's House of Commons. Upon his return, he was asked during "Question Time" by an opposition party member what he thought of the game.

A Parliamentary correspondent pal of mine, who claims to have been present, recalled that the great man took his time wrestling himself up off the front bench out of a semi-doze and hauling his massive bulk erect, whereupon he intoned: "Golf is a game that consists of getting a very small ball into an even smaller hole with implements singularly ill-designed for the purpose."

Rosemarie Jarski, in her hilarious little book *Great British Wit*, writes that the old statesman's words were: "Golf is an ineffectual attempt to direct an uncontrollable sphere into an inaccessible hole with instruments ill-adapted to the purpose."

Whichever—and there are other versions, also—the description was a classic example of the man's superb command of the language.

In addition, of course, to being the truth!

Nothing to do with golf, but here are a couple more of my favorite examples of Churchillian rapier wit and verbal deftness, both in response to his famed longtime social adversary, Lady Nancy Astor:

Lady Astor: "Churchill, if I were married to you, I would put arsenic in your tea."

Churchill: "And, madam, if I were married to you, I would drink it."

Lady Astor: "Churchill, you are drunk!"

Churchill: "Yes, madam, and you are ugly. But tomorrow I will be sober."

forty-five

"WELL, IF YOU WERE TO..."

I must have heard a million golf jokes. Only a few of them were really funny. Here's my favorite. The guy who told it to me swears it's not a joke but the truth. I wouldn't bet against that, but you decide.

Four buddies are playing their regular Saturday round when one of them, named Bloggs, hits the emperor of all slices, whaling his tee shot over an OB fence and the thickets of bushes and trees beyond it toward a major highway paralleling the hole they were playing. The guy cusses, reloads, gets the second ball in play, makes a quad, cusses some more, and on they go.

A couple of holes later, as the four are putting out, here comes the pro, racing up in a cart. Leaping out, face ashen, he hustles up to the group and blurts, "Gentleman, I'm awfully sorry, but we have an extremely serious problem. Please tell me who hit that tee shot out of bounds on 13."

His friends immediately turn to Bloggsy, leaving him with no option but to raise a hand. Doing so, he growls, "So what? I've done it a thousand times."

The pro steps closer to him.

"Mr. Bloggs, I have some terrible news. You see, this time your ball must have cleared the trees, because the police are here and they say a golf ball went clean through a tour bus windshield out there on the highway, and that the driver lost control and crossed the divide and clipped a truck, which rammed into a car, which slewed off and hit two more cars..."

Getting to the worst part, the pro brushes back his hair with a trembling hand.

"And, well, there are five people on the way to the hospital, and more needing medical attention, and one old lady's gone into shock and keeps taking off her clothes…and…and…Well, it's just an awful, *awful* situation."

Eyes widening, mouth dropping, face graying, blinking furiously, Bloggsy claps both hands to his forehead.

"Lord Almighty! How could I have done such a thing? What a terrible, terrible…" Then, as the shock sinks in, his voice peters out. But a moment later, trying to gather himself, he grabs the pro's arm and says, "Jimmy, Jimmy, I'm at a complete loss. What do you think I should *do*?"

Freeing himself from his member's grip, the pro reaches out and gently grasps Bloggsy's trembling left hand.

"Well," he says, "if you were to position this hand when you take your grip just a *little* more on top of the shaft—like, strengthen it a *little*—I really do think it would help you enormously with that horrible slice of yours…"

forty-six

"JUST *Too* DAMN FRUSTRATING!"

Y ou're not going to believe what follows, but I swear it's true. There has long been an abundance of eccentricity in British golf clubs, and especially the more "up-market" establishments. The prime example I ever experienced was at an elite little club of the lovely pine-and-heather variety located not far out of London.

Visiting with a member one idyllic spring day, I was disembarking his vehicle when into the car park (sorry, parking lot) rolled a beautifully maintained antique Rolls Royce that eventually meandered to a stop perhaps 50 yards away. The spot was not within any defined parking area, but provided its occupants with privacy plus a spectacular view down one of the course's prettiest holes.

"Watch," said my host, indicating I should do so unobserved by getting back in his car.

After a few seconds, a hard-faced, middle-aged man emerged with great dignity from the Rolls's driver's seat, immaculately clad from head to toe in what Hollywood might have cooked up as the uniform of a Victorian-era horse-and-carriage driver. Moving to the rear of the Rolls, the chauffeur proceeded slowly to open the vehicle's "boot" (trunk), then carefully withdraw from it and set up alongside the rear passenger door an elegant picnic table and matching chair. Next, he covered the table with a fine linen cloth, fetched from the boot and set in place some expensive china and flatware, then carefully carried over, unwrapped, and appropriately arranged on the table the elements of what clearly was to be his master's lunch.

These tasks completed, the chauffeur turned to and, with a slight flourish, opened the Rolls's rear passenger door, after which, following a small bow, he gently took the elbow of an elderly man clad in a Tattersal checked shirt, a regimental-type striped tie, a beautifully fitted plus-four suit, and a pair of exquisitely polished brown brogue golf shoes. With a nod and a smile to his servant, the passenger disembarked, carefully seated himself at the picnic table, then, with a further nod of approval, picked up a knife and fork and began his repast.

"Who and what the heck—" I started to say, when my host raised a hand to stop me.

"A very distinguished lord of the realm." he murmured, "and, of course, a highly respected member of our club. And if you think eating his lunch out here is a little odd, wait until you see what happens when he's finished. We'll try to get off right behind them so you can watch. But, if they spot us, you must promise to appear to take what you're seeing as simply a matter of course. No approaching them, otherwise, Danny—that's the chauffeur's name—might get a little fractious, and he's a former Irish middleweight champion. So just a smile and a wave at the most, okay?"

Cut to my pal and I killing time on the putting green as the old gentleman, suitably fed, rounds the corner of the clubhouse followed by Danny, who is now carrying under one arm a slim canvas golf bag containing perhaps a half set of clubs.

"Never enters the clubhouse," whispers my pal. "But here we go—watch this."

The nearby 1st tee is clear, and, as Lord Whomever walks on to it, he silently extends a hand behind him, into which his man quickly places what appears to be a driver that Old Tom Morris might have used in winning one of his four British Opens back in the 1860s: thickly leather-wrapped grip, highly polished hickory shaft, tiny pear-shaped wooden head.

After sniffing the air a couple of times as he stares down the fairway, I watch as his lordship makes a couple of short and easy practice swings, then half turns his head and says something to his servant. By then, my host and I have practice-putted our balls sufficiently close to the tee to be able to hear the reply, voiced in a heavy Irish brogue: "Indeed, m'lord, it surely is a foine afternoon. And I have a feelin' that's goin' to help youse play verra nicely today, that I do."

"Well," says the old man with a slight smile, "we'll soon see."

Whereupon, Lord Whomever walks to the center of the tee, assumes a workmanlike golf stance, waggles his ancient driver's head a couple of times, takes a final glance down the fairway, and makes a swing about twice as long and fast as his warm-up efforts. Then, while holding his follow-through and frowning, he turns his head to stare into the abundant right rough.

"Damn!" he says. "Pushed the damn thing again. Same old fault, same old fault. Thought I'd found the answer to that the other day, but clearly not."

By this point my mouth is hanging open in awe and wonder. Eventually, I manage to whisper to my buddy, "Is what I'm seeing *really* what I'm seeing?"

"Thought you'd be surprised—a little different, isn't it?" he replies with a big grin.

"No ball," I say.

"Exactly. Golf played without a ball," he confirms.

Cut to a few minutes later with the pair of us standing behind our drives, studying his lordship's stately progress down the opening hole.

After the no-ball drive, this no-ball golfer and his Danny boy amble maybe a couple hundred yards into the right rough, where the old man momentarily studies his non-ball in the tall grass, then makes a couple of easy practice swings, before—as *he* sees it, at least—firing for real. Seconds later, he raises his club in self-salute to himself as his non-approach shot apparently lands on the putting surface.

But my mouth by then has fallen much too far open to emit words as, dumbstruck, I watch him walk onto the green, reach into his jacket pocket, extract a golf ball, drop it about 30 feet from the hole, hold out his hand to his man for his putter, receive it, momentarily plumb-bob, then quickly two-putt for...what?

Nodding to himself, my host says, "That's a par, I'm sure."

There's quite a lengthy silence before I inquire, "And it's like that all the time?"

"Without fail. Three or four days a week in summer when the weather's decent. Lunch in the parking lot, nine holes without hitting a ball except for putting, then back in the Roller and off home."

I let a few more seconds of sinking-in time pass, then, as my pal pulls a club for his approach shot, question him again.

"Has anyone ever asked him, well...*why?*"

My friend hits his shot solidly, watches the ball fly, then grimaces as it comes up a few yards short.

"Yes, in fact they have. Our captain at the time, another lord— apparently they sit together in the House sometimes—did a few years ago. Our non-ball man was very pleasant about it. Said he liked the exercise and the fresh air, but that to play the game with a ball—except for put- ting—had become just 'too, *too* damn frustrating.'

"So he'd given up on it. And, he insisted, was now a great deal happier with the game."

Note: People to whom I've told this story seemed to enjoy it, though many refused to believe it. I swear on my favorite driver that it's true.

part four

EXPERIENCES

forty-seven

WHINE AT YOUR PERIL

Players apart, there probably has never been a bigger deal in American golf than Joseph C. Dey Jr.

Born in Norfolk, Virginia, in 1907 to a patrician family, Joe, as his legions of friends called him, considered studying for the ministry following graduation from the University of Pennsylvania, but instead began his working life as a Philadelphia sportswriter. From 1934 through 1968 he served as the increasingly exalted executive director of the United States Golf Association, during which time he played a leading role in launching five new national championships and a couple of esteemed international tournaments. In 1969, more or less in response to popular demand, he became the first Commissioner of the PGA Tour after the tournament players broke away from the PGA of America and needed a strong, astute, and highly respected leader, holding that position until 1974. He was the instigator of what is now known as the Players Championship, in 1975 became one of only three Americans to captain the Royal and Ancient Golf Club of St. Andrews, and through 2007 was the only non-player designated as an honoree of his great friend Jack Nicklaus's Memorial Tournament a little over a year after his death at age 83. If anyone ever existed who knew and cared more about the Rules of Golf, they could be numbered on the fingers of less than one hand.

For much of his life Joe lived on New York's Long Island, where he was a highly regarded—indeed, iconic—member of the ultra-exclusive but extremely enjoyable Creek Club. I was, accordingly, delighted when, during a guest-editor spell at *Golf Digest*, he invited me to join him and a couple of other friends for a game there.

It was a gorgeous summer day, I was playing well, and early in the round, after an excellent tee shot, I became so infuriated after dumping a short-iron approach in a bunker that, despite my nervousness about in any way upsetting my distinguished host, I simply could not hold back a brief burst of self-abuse.

No obscenities were involved in front of so highly religious a man, but, clearly from the expression on his face, the outburst definitely displeased Joe Dey. Nevertheless, for some minutes he held his counsel, until, as we neared the green together, he came close and gently put his arm around my shoulders. Then, quietly enough for our companions not to hear, he spoke some words that will remain with me forever.

"Young fellow," he said, "I think I should inform you that at this club we have an unusual rule, that being every whine about a mis-hit mandates a $10 contribution to the poor box at the completion of the round."

I can assure you that there was definitely no more whining from a distinctly subdued golf writer for the rest of that day. Joe's admonition also initiated my habit of applying fines for whines to golfing buddies, at rates of $2, $5, and $10, depending on the severity of the offense.

I keep the poor box, which presently contains quite a handsome sum—unfortunately, almost all of it contributed by yours truly.

forty-eight

TOUCHES OF SCOTLAND

Among golf historians controversy continues, as it has for centuries, about where the game originated, although no one disputes that it evolved into the form we know today in Scotland, with St. Andrews the focal point.

Here's my "take" on the matter.

Many years ago I spent Hogmany (the New Year's holiday unless you're Scottish) as a guest of some friends in that fair nation's far north, way up above even the glorious Royal Dornoch. The weather was atrocious—bitterly cold with deep snow and howling winds—but did not stop my devout hosts from attending their usual Sunday morning church service, nor from insisting that I accompany them. I was warned, however, to dress extra warmly, as the ancient little stone "kirk" they worshipped in was unheated.

Wearing just about all of the clothing I'd traveled with, plus a borrowed heavy overcoat and a monster muffler, I managed to get through the early part of the service without my teeth chattering. But the climax came in the form of a marathon sermon by the most hellfire-and-damnation preacher I've ever heard, by the end of which I knew what a block of ice must feel like.

As I somehow managed to stagger to my feet in preparation for exiting the building, it occurred to me that only people prepared to suffer through such experiences could have invented as unrelentingly a punitive game as golf, and I lightly mentioned the thought to an amiable-looking old fellow also easing his way out of the holy refrigerator.

"Aye," he said, with a nod and a grin. "Weel, most of the folk up here were devoted Calvinists back then. There's few left now, but that was a Calvinist service ye just attended."

Puzzled, I asked him what that had to do with my observation about golf.

"Och aye," he said with a twinkle in his eye. "Didya nae know, laddie, that to a good Calvinist any form of pleasure is sinful?"

Arriving by chance in the far-northern village of Dornoch while roaming our beloved Caledonia one summer, Jean and I checked into the first hotel we came to, an old manor-house-type building at slightly run-down peace with itself in grounds riotous with wild flowers and giant trees.

The room we were allotted was creakily but comfortably furnished; dinner ran five superb homemade courses for what at the Old Course Hotel or Pebble Beach might have bought you a cup of coffee and a cookie; and it was light enough late enough to walk off the feast with a round (in our case, the second of the day) on the famous course. Upon our return close to midnight, we found that the proprietor had retired, but, as was his custom, had left the bar open on the "honor" system for guests fancying a late whistle-wetter (or two or three, as in the case of our more lively fellow residents!).

Late the evening of our third day we stopped the owner—bekilted as usual—on his way out the bar to explain that we had an extremely early flight from Inverness the next morning on our way back across the pond, must therefore depart the hotel in the wee hours, and asked him to kindly tot up our tab for immediate settlement.

"Och aye," he said with a shrug. "It's much too late for all that noo, and we have your address in America, I'm sure. So just be on your way with our thanks and good wishes and we'll send the bill on to you."

A month passed, then two, then three, and we were coming up for four when a simple handwritten invoice arrived for an extremely fair amount, with a message scribbled on the back: "It was great having you. Will ye nae come back and see us soon?"

More and more, we ask ourselves where else in this 21st-century world something like that could happen.

Back before the British Open grew to its present majestic or monolithic proportions (your choice), I always made a point of catching a particular sideshow when covering the game's oldest championship at St. Andrews, Scotland's famed "Home of Golf."

In those days, as the great professionals competed over the Old Course, you could watch a seemingly endless procession of "trolley"-pulling or bag-toting everyday bangers and bunters going about their appointed rounds on the adjoining New and Eden courses, mostly with barely a glance at the extravaganza occurring sometimes no more than a pitch shot distant from them.

Observing that scene confirmed two factors about the game that I believed true then and still do.

The first is that golf's appeal lies infinitely more in playing the game than watching it being played, no matter how well. Growing out of that, the second is the absolute irrelevance of high-level tournament play to golf's ongoing health as an everyman (and woman) recreational activity.

Or, as an editorialist once commented in the *Times* of London during the championship week: "If all of the world's professional tours and tourists vanished overnight, grassroots golfers might bow their heads momentarily in respectful farewell, but would then get on with playing the game themselves without giving their disappearance another thought."

That will never happen, of course. But it remains an intriguing scenario.

forty-nine

PREMONITION

According to the mind-menders, most people have premonitions, meaning forewarnings of future happenings.

Most of mine have been wrong, with one notable exception.

In the 1993 Memorial Tournament, Paul Azinger came to the last hole at Muirfield Village needing a birdie for the chance to tie Payne Stewart, his best pal on tour, and possibly force a playoff. But both players hit their second shots at the tough par 4 into the deep bunker left of the green.

Playing first from an unfortunate plugged lie, Stewart—who'd finished second and twice third in his last four Memorials—hit a magnificent recovery to eight feet above the hole, leaving him an excellent chance at what the thousands watching in the flesh and on TV surely assumed would be a winning par.

I was working in ABC Sports' 18th-hole camera tower with tournament founder and host Jack Nicklaus and the ace commentator Jack Whitaker. As Azinger set up to his by-no-means-easy bunker shot, a little internal voice suddenly told me, "He's going to hole it!" Before I could stop myself, I'd blurted the words aloud.

Putting his hand over his microphone, Nicklaus said, "Get out of here!"—or maybe something a little racier. Whitaker just looked at me in amazement.

Azinger wasted no time setting up to his shot, swung, and just cleared the bunker lip with the ball, which then ran some 15 feet across the green before lazily plopping into the cup.

Sinking to his knees, Azinger raised his arms and the club high, his expression a mixture of surprise and elation. When the even more shocked Stewart 3-putted from eight feet moments later, Azinger had won the Memorial from Corey Pavin.

Nicklaus gave me a sideways look of wonderment, and, as the crowd uproar waned, Whitaker murmured, "Didn't know you were psychic."

Denouement.

When Azinger finally got to the locker room to pick up his golf shoes following all the celebrations, he found them stuffed with mashed bananas—a classic example of his victim's sense of humor. Stewart—who tragically died in a plane crash six years later—showed further grace by going to a nearby inn, where he bought drinks for tournament workers and held the bar for a decidedly riotous limbo contest.

fifty

MEMORIAL HIGHS...
AND LOWS

I was fortunate to be part of a team that helped Jack Nicklaus create his Memorial Tournament in the early 1970s, then served as an executive committee member, captain of Muirfield Village Golf Club, and editorial director of the event's annual publication, the *Memorial Magazine*, through the 2006 tournament.

Judging by the superlative condition, beauty, and challenge of the course, the quality of the fields, the players' frequently voiced laudations of how they are treated each year—the milk shakes in particular had become a massive hit—and the "sellout" fan attendances, the Memorial has grown into one of the world's premier golf tournaments.

Here are a few of my most vivid memories from an invariably memorable event.

- First-time winner in 1974 Roger Maltbie's hideous last-day pants, featuring giant plaid patches (believe it or not, such garments were all the rage among golfers at that time). The pants didn't stop Maltbie from defeating Hale Irwin in a three-hole playoff after bouncing a wild approach shot off a skinny metal gallery stake onto the 17th green for a critical 2-putt par. Maltbie brought the stake to the winner's news conference, then celebrated hard enough to mislay his $40,000 winner's check in a bar (the 2007 winner got $1,080,000!). Maltbie, incidentally, had won with clubs loaned to him by Lee Trevino that he'd used for only a couple of weeks.
- Founder and host Jack Nicklaus being so thrilled by his 1977 win that he came very close to announcing his retirement from tourna-

ment play. His wife Barbara talked him out of it, and many success-ful years passed for the Bear before he finally hung 'em up at the 2005 British Open at St. Andrews in Scotland.

- The absolute worst of the tournament's litany of bad weather in 1979's second round, consisting of 35 mph winds and 40-degree tem-peratures dropping the wind-chill factor to 13 degrees. The field's average score was 79.4, with first-year winner Maltbie returning a tournament-record high 92, including 50 whacks on the back nine. But the day remains most memorable for eventual winner Tom Watson completing one of golf's all-time great rounds when, heavily bundled in sweaters and rain gear, he somehow returned a bogey-free 3-under-par 69.

- Sam Snead playing with Arnold Palmer and Gary Player in round one in 1982—the year an on course beer cost 75¢!—after the first-tee gallery serenaded the Slammer with "Happy Birthday" on his 70th. Also that year, Jodie Mudd winning a long-drive contest with a 314-yard smash using a wooden-headed driver. (Only a decade later, John Daly, using steel-headed "woods," was threatening cars on Memorial Drive located 350-plus-yards from the same practice-range tees.)

- Scott Hoch's comment on choking following his 1983 meltdown final round of 78, after leading by 4 at its start, when asked if he'd like a drink: "I hope my throat is big enough now so I can get it down."

- Nicklaus fans cheering in 1984 when Andy Bean bunkered a shot, then missed a two-foot birdie putt, to allow Jack to become the first two-time Memorial winner in the event's second playoff. Those crowd reactions upset Nicklaus, but Bean took them well. "You're in the Bear's den here," he said, "so I guess it's going to be that way." Jack had stunningly push-sliced his tee shot way out of bounds at number 17 in the final round, but then holed a 25-foot putt for bogey with his second ball to remain tied with Bean.

- Lanny Wadkins missing a 15-inch par putt at 9 in 1985's final round before losing to the next two-time winner, Hale Irwin, by a stroke. (Greg Norman and Tom Watson also won twice, and Tiger Woods three times consecutively.)

- Almost an inch of snow falling on the Monday of tournament week in 1989, with, thereafter, below-average temperatures and rain severely impacting play. The following year, high winds on day one forced grounding of the TV broadcaster's blimp, and 40 players scored into the 80s.
- Sick of such weather problems, in 1993 Barbara Nicklaus—at Arnold Palmer's first wife Winnie's suggestion, and accompanied by then general chairman Pandel Savic—placing a shot of gin on the tombstone of local Indian chief Leatherlips, rumored to have laid a bad-weather curse on the tournament because of the course being built near his burial ground. It stopped raining before she and Savic left the site—but only briefly.
- Also in 1993 Bobby Wadkins making the Memorial's first double-eagle, after 5,891 Memorial rounds, by holing a 3-wood shot from 237 yards at the par-5 15th hole.
- Playing with a never-before-used wooden-headed driver he'd dug out of his garage, Tom Lehman winning the 1994 tournament with four immaculate 67s for the still-record Memorial 72-hole score of 268.
- In 1995 Greg Norman 1-putting six of the last seven greens to win. Also, the courage and grace that year of defending champion Paul Azinger appearing at the tournament, although bald-headed and unable to play because of chemotherapy treatment for shoulder cancer.
- Tiger Woods's third straight victory in 2001 with a final round 66 to win by a still, as I write, tournament record 7 strokes.
- Two years later, George H.W. Bush declining an invitation from Woods to join him on the practice range before a corporate pro-am. "No thanks," said Number 41. "I just don't need the humiliation."
- In a year of decent weather, caddie Craig "Woody" Camoroli winning a $100 dare by eating a live cicada during the 2004 invasion of central Ohio by the once-every-17-years bugs. Also that year, Ernie Els 1-putting 11 of his last 14 holes to defeat 1998 winner Fred Couples with a tournament-record-low total of 100 putts.
- Journeyman Bart Bryant's superb final-hole third shot and gutsy par-saving and winning 14-foot putt, after being forced to take a drop and

penalty stroke off his drive, for his second PGA Tour victory after waiting 18 years for his first.

- South African player Fulton Allem driving one of the tournament's brand-new courtesy cars to Texas after a Memorial Tournament. It took a week for officials to find it, whereupon one had to fly south then drive it back to Ohio. Said Allem innocuously, "I thought I could have it indefinitely."

fifty-one

SHOWBIZ GOLF

From 1974 through 1993, a company called TelEvents coproduced a total of 199 50-minute golf-based entertainment programs, primarily with the BBC, plus a few later shows airing on the British commercial network Channel 4.

I was a 50 percent owner and co–chief executive of that company with my Golden Bear International colleague and great friend, David Sherman. Headquartered in London, the firm was headed there initially by an entrepreneurial former ad man by the name of James Wotton, and latterly by a delightful member of what by then remained of British "society" named Caroline Brooman-White.

One hundred and eighty-seven of our programs consisted of a series of "pro-celebrity" matches that featured top professionals leading teams of amateurs—mostly top-name entertainers and athletes from other sports. Our first series totaled seven shows, with the remaining series numbering 10 programs each. All were videotaped in full by the broadcasters, then edited into 50-minute programs for autumn and winter evening broadcast. Not least because of their prime-time airings, many of the shows drew bigger audiences than each summer's live British Open telecasts.

Eight of the series were shot at Gleneagles and seven at Turnberry, Scotland's primary and legendary golf resorts. One was made at Le Touquet in northern France, two at the Dromoland Castle resort in western Ireland, and the final program back in golf's home country at the Loch Lomond Golf Club.

In the early 1980s TelEvents also packaged for the BBC—at the suggestion of its then head, Bill Cotton—four six-part series featuring top men professionals competing against their female equivalents at Woburn

Golf and Country Club in southern England. Featured were Joanne Carner, Beth Daniel, Sandra Haynie, Sally Little, Nancy Lopez, and Jan Stephenson, along with Seve Ballesteros, Bernhard Langer, Johnny Miller, Greg Norman, and Jerry Pate.

In 1979 TelEvents coproduced three programs for the BBC titled *Jack Nicklaus at the Home of Golf*, starring the world's number one golfer along with friends Glen Campbell, Sean Connery, and Ben Crenshaw. The shows featured, among other elements, the quartet playing St. Andrews's Old Course and a tour of the Royal and Ancient Golf Club and its famed clubhouse and many historic artifacts hosted by proud member Connery.

Following are some of the most and least amusing high- and lowlights of those "showbiz" experiences.

LOWLIGHTS

As just mentioned, the amateur participants in our pro-celebrity golf shows were top-line entertainers—primarily American and British actors and comedians—plus largely European star professional athletes.

Our problems with the athletes were relatively minimal, but my stomach still hurts when I think back to some of the hiccups we had with show-business types.

A complete telling would fill most of this book, so here's just a sampling:

An associate informed me that a notoriously irascible five-star American actor had just arrived, was hitting balls on the range in the rain (very badly), and didn't seem deliriously happy to have joined us. Accordingly, my colleague suggested I go down and try to brighten him up.

Following my greeting, which included a few words about how delighted we were the superstar was participating, he said nothing while shanking a couple more balls, then stopped and leaned on the club as the following dialog ensued:

Actor (ruminatively): "I think I just stepped on my cock."

Me (after a few seconds recovering from shock): "Oh dear. That must have been extremely painful. How did you manage it?"

Actor: "By coming here."

Me: "Well, now that you have, I hope you enjoy yourself."

Actor (knowing he was scheduled to play his match the next afternoon): "I'll probably leave in the morning."

Me: "That would make us very sad. But is there anything we can do for you in the meantime?"

Actor: "Yeah. Bug off."

Returning to the hotel, something I'd heard about the fellow occurred to me, and I quickly tracked down his "significant other" in our hospitality suite. Surprising homely for the companion of so titanic a Hollywood "name," she seemed both a nice woman and no dummy, because, after we introduced ourselves, she said, with a frown, "He's not happy, right?"

Me: "That, ma'am, is a definite understatement."

She: "Well, I suggest you get some booze in him quick as you can. A couple of gin martinis. Large. Light on the vermouth."

Me: "I hope our barman can make them to his liking."

She, after a moment's reflection: "Listen, forget that. When he gets in here I'll take him behind the bar and let him fix his own. Just set that up for me, will you?"

Which I did, and she did, and he did—in a large water tumbler, still sopping wet from the range—and quickly chugalugged. Whereupon, an hour or so later, the guy actually smiled at me as he said on their way out of the room, "One o'clock camera call tomorrow, right?"

And his game sort of came around, too—only three shanks in the nine holes.

"Sir," said the five-star hotel's manager, more puzzled than distraught, "one of *your people* has demanded 20 bed sheets with which he's covered the entire flooring of his suite. Do you have any idea *why?*"

I responded that I did not, but would try to find out when I accompanied this renowned thespian in his practice round later that day. After a few holes, which he played surprisingly well, I managed to make the inquiry very offhandedly and with an understanding grin.

His response: "Because my wife says the carpets are just too filthy to walk on in her bare feet, which means I've had to carry her to and from the bathroom. And, as you know having met her, she's no featherweight."

Wondering why a probable multimillionairess hadn't packed or bought a pair of slippers, I seem to remember that my reply was simply, "Oh." What I'm sure of is lying to the manager that I hadn't managed to pluck up the nerve to ask the guy about the darn sheets.

A third American superstar of film and stage, who also enjoyed his "see-through yum-yums," and accompanied them with small cigars, had staggered off to bed around midnight, but then reappeared in the hospitality suite not many minutes later.

"Ah need a...ugh...doctor," he slurred at me, and naturally I inquired as to why.

"Well," he gradually got out, "Ah had to take a dump, see? And then ah drop my f*cking cigar in the john and it sets fire to the paper ah'd just used. And, goddamn it, the flames burn my ass, so ah yell as ah jump up and run into the bedroom."

Pulling every ounce of self control I possessed into keeping a straight face, I asked, "You mean you need treatment for your...er, well, inflamed posterior?"

"Hell no," groaned the actor. "Me yellin' woke up my wife, which made her so f*cking mad she tried to whap me."

Still working on self-control, I started to respond, "I'm sorry, but I don't quite understand—"

"Look, she missed me with the swat, but then she grabs my hand and wrenches on it, and ah think she busted my f*cking thumb. Hurts like hell, anyway. Definitely need...ugh, ugh...a goddamn doctor."

We sat him down and fed him some consoling words, plus another large see-through yum-yum, and finally persuaded him to risk facing his dearly beloved again, which eventually he staggered off to do.

His thumb still hurt the next day, he told me, but not as bad as his head and his "f*cking ass."

Actor number four was famed in film then later even more in a hugely popular TV series. As with all our American stars, he was invited to bring one guest, with both parties traveling from California and back first-class at our expense.

The guy eventually arrived at the hotel in one of our chauffeured Rolls-Royce limos, which was filled to bursting. Behind it trailed a taxi in the same condition. Wifey was not among the entourage, but a gorgeous girlfriend maybe a third our man's age was, plus his brother and, we assume, every lackey employed on his personal Hollywood servicing team. And all were traveling and staying on our tab, of course.

Somehow we found rooms for this unexpected (and very much unwanted) retinue, but the biggest problem proved to be the brother. Apparently possessed of theatrical aspirations, and clearly desperate for equal visibility with his star sibling, he insisted on standing within a few feet of the big cheese during the show's taping, greens included, meaning he would be on camera in every take. Finally, it took a threat of physical ejection from our giant ex-cop stage manager to get and keep the idiot out of the show.

A rock superstar is the focus of the next story, flown in by private jet at our expense from a gig on the Continent, after agreeing to play the following morning.

With the aid of his entourage, the guy somehow managed to squirrel his way to his suite minus contact with any of our team, so the first we heard from him was that he'd gotten some kind of really bad bug and was suddenly way too sick to even think about playing golf.

Suspicious, I won a war with his entourage members about making personal contact, whereupon it quickly became clear that the man was either bombed out of his mind or severely stoned, or most likely both. And this was one we lost, because, whatever the cause of his condition, there was no way he could have even balanced a ball on a tee within at least the next 24 hours.

Many years later the rocker, by then a low-handicapper, admitted to an interviewer that, back at the time he was supposed to play for us, he was drinking a quart of whiskey and a half case of beer a day. "I would vomit blood and then reach for the bottle," he was quoted as saying. "I was going to die." Then, as he put it, "I traded one addiction for another. Golf is the crack of sports. Once I took it seriously, I loved it, and I've never tired of playing. And it saved my life."

I congratulate him but just wish the metamorphosis had happened earlier—because the incident sure did zero for my life.

Along the same lines—different years but the same syndrome—comes stage fright.

Although expressing delight at being invited weeks ahead of time, and enjoying their pre-shoot partying, when the time comes to roll videotape, a renowned four-handicap balladeer and a sometime world tennis ace each become so terrified of exposing their so-called golf to the world that they upchuck in the gorse bushes. That, of course, in addition to playing appallingly badly.

Back to the actors for a couple of quickies:

- Famed movie tough-guy, playing in stony silence, when requested to interact verbally with his pro and opponents: "If you want me to f*cking talk, gimme a f*cking script."
- Another A-list actor, claiming a reasonable handicap upon receiving an invitation, arrives minus clubs, wants us to buy him a set, finally agrees to make do with loaners, but shows up for his match in high-heeled cowboy boots. Watching him make supposed practice swings, my belly does somersaults, yet somehow the guy miraculously bogeys the opening hole, a par 3. But then he dribbles his tee shot into a fairway bunker at the next one, where, boots sunk deep in the sand, he calls plaintively to his British Open–winner professional partner, "Hey, ace, what do I do now? Get over here and help me, 'cuz I've never played this crazy game before."

That earned me a distinctly unpleasant interview with the BBC second channel's top man of the time, who was supposed to be paying us a friendly visit.

Even worse, the non-golfer had the gall to hang around for the rest of the week, satisfying a mighty thirst.

But here's the topper.

The perpetrator: one of America's all-time titans of both film and theater, but a man who unashamedly informs dinner guests, as he unremittingly alternates undiluted and uniced vodka with beer throughout the evenings (and the days too, presumably): "I can still work because I'm that rarity, a fully functioning alcoholic."

Bing Crosby was topping our bill this time around, and had been asked by the head man of a major charity dinner organized to open our week as chair of that event. But, no lover of pomp and circumstance, on the night of the wing-ding, the legendary crooner, still jet-lagged and with a TV match early the next morning, decided to opt out in favor of a pint with the locals down at a village pub, then early to bed.

Chaos ensued, of course, until, unbeknownst to us, our sponsor's representative, deciding (erroneously) that the aforementioned functioning alcoholic was the next biggest star present, invited him to sit in for Bing. Still clad in the revolting plaid pants and beat-up orange nylon windbreaker he'd worn for an afternoon practice round, followed by a couple of hours imbibing in the hospitality suite, this he did. Almost everyone else present was in evening dress.

Seated at a down-room table and busily hosting more of our celebrities, my pre-first-course chore was to further pacify the actor who'd claimed to have stepped on a private part before gin and vermouth apparently healed both that and his psyche. This was going swimmingly until, suddenly gazing around, the superstar spotted his orange-jacketed fellow thespian seated in the place of honor at the center of the elevated head table.

Oh boy!

His face becoming a mask of rage, up jumped my—as I by then thought—totally becalmed one, knocking his chair flying as he proceeded in great haste towards Bing's replacement. Concerned about what might be about to happen, I trotted a foot behind him.

Arriving face to face with Orange Jacket, he then unleashed approximately the following:

"Jesus Christ Almighty! What the f*ck is a goddamned B-class actor and no-good bum like you doing sitting up there as though you own this f*cking joint—and especially in those crappy clothes and probably drunk as a stinking skunk as usual? God, who in hell invited you of all people over here, anyway?"—etcetera, etcetera, etcetera. At the end of which, Orange Jacket, without uttering a word—I later figured he was probably incapable of so doing—regarded his attacker blearily for a long moment, slugged back the remainder of a tumbler's worth of warm vodka, shakily raised a single finger to my supposedly becalmed one, lurched up, and, with as much dignity as he could muster in his extremely unsteady condition, departed the huge ballroom.

Cut to 5:45 the next morning.

My wife and I were both deeply asleep when the phone rang and the familiar voice of the hotel's night porter somewhat shakily uttered the following: "Mr. Bowden, sir, I am terribly sorry to disturb you so early, but I'm in your hospitality suite, where one of your celebrity gentlemen is lying on the floor. I've tried to arouse him, but unsuccessfully, I'm sorry to say. In fact, it appears to me that he might be…Well, sir, quite possibly, er…*dead*, sir. So would you mind awfully coming down and…" etcetera, etcetera.

I threw a sweater and pants over my T-shirt and boxers and was there in what felt like a few seconds.

Orange Jacket was, indeed, sprawled on the floor in front of the bar, and, even from the distance of a few feet, really did look as though he might have bought the farm. Getting on my hands and knees, I felt his wrist and neck for a pulse, and almost passed out with relief when one faintly registered. Whereupon the night porter and I began trying to revive the guy by slapping his face, then, when that failed, soaking a big bar towel in ice water and slopping it around his horribly bloated visage.

After perhaps a couple of minutes of this, the body emitted a faint groan, whereupon we slapped and slopped harder. A minute or two more and the eyes blinked partially open, and what sounded like an attempt at words emerged.

Getting as close as I could to Orange Jacket's closest ear, I asked him what he was trying to say. After four or five more unintelligible efforts, finally it came through. He wanted to "take a leak."

Somehow or other, the porter and I got the man more or less upright, then slowly—he collapsed three times—propelled him to the lobby men's room. Therein at a stall, with some embarrassment, we prepared him to do as he said he wished, only to spend some minutes holding him erect and correctly aimed, but with no action forthcoming from his waterworks. Finally, I told the porter to drum up sufficient help to get the man to his suite, undress as much of him as possible, and dump the rest in a cold bath.

This exercise took a while but was finally achieved, whereupon the porter called to inform me that Orange Jacket had finally come around to a point where the dousing crew felt he could be left to his own devices.

I returned to my room where I showered and dressed more appropriately, then phoned Orange Jacket. After about 12 rings, a near-human voice mumbled something that might have been "Yuh?"

Identifying myself, I asked if there was anything we could do for him.

There was a lengthy silence, followed by the "Yuh" sound again, followed by what, on the third repeat, I'm pretty certain I identified as the words, "Wanna go home."

"You want to go home?" I asked, to be sure.

"Yuh."

"Where's home?"

Grunt, then, "'Merica."

"Yes, I know that," I respond. "But it's quite a large country, right? So anywhere *particular* in America?"

A long pause, during which he was probably trying to remember where he lived. Then, "Jus' 'Merica. Any goddamn place. An' now. Right *now.*"

Which is when I snapped.

With the help of an associate, over the course of the next hour it was arranged for Orange Jacket to be limoed to the nearest major airport, from where, leaving late that morning, he would be flown to New York City.

With everything in place, I called his room and told him—as I recall, four times at least—what had been set up and by what time he must make it to the lobby to leave.

The time came, and the man descended the stairs slowly, but at least by foot rather than rolling. He was still in the plaid pants and the orange wind breaker. What he didn't have was luggage.

As we escorted him to the door, then to the "Roller"—as our long-time head driver, John Wells, always called it—John asked me what he should do if there was any "trouble" with his passenger on the drive to the airport.

"John," I replied, "you once told me you were both a pro boxer and a 'minder' for a big-time London bad boy in an earlier life, so I'll leave that to you." With a smile that clearly expressed his hope that there would, indeed, be trouble, Wells answered, "Right, guv'nor. Just leave 'im to me."

As Orange Jacket was assisted into the car, our company's European chief, who'd been questioning the appropriate hotel staffers on the subject, piped up, "Look, sir, you don't appear to have any luggage and I know you came with a lot. What do you want us to do about that?"

Orange Jacket's two-word reply will live with all of us forever.
"Burn it," he said.

Which we did—and sent him the ashes in an extremely unattractive
little urn.

HIGHLIGHTS

Anyone hugely or even middlingly famous as an entertainer, a mass com-
municator, or a sports figure from 1974 through 1993 who loved golf,
could break 100, and speak some semblance of English was a candidate
for our pro-celebrity series.

That produced an extraordinarily rich mix of high achievers and beguil-
ing personalities, almost all of whom—despite the immediate foregoing—
generally behaved impeccably at what invariably assumed and sustained
the character of large upscale house-parties. Through the generosity of
our corporate sponsors, this was made possible by our taking over for each
week of shooting major portions of the aforementioned and other
renowned hotels featuring five-star hospitality suite setups, exceptional
food service, triple-A staff cooperation, all the golf even the most severely
addicted of our guests could play on superb courses, plus unlimited use
of each resort's other sports and recreational facilities.

Indeed, so enjoyable did participation become that, after the first two
series spread the word, numbers of "celebs" would contact our primary
London executives early each year regarding shooting dates to ensure
their availability if invited—or even, in some cases, bluntly solicit
appearances.

Among the American showbiz stars everyone especially enjoyed
socially were, alphabetically, Glen Campbell, Richard Crenna, Bing
Crosby, Peter Falk, Phil Harris, Howard Keel, Fred MacMurray, Dick
Martin, astronaut and moon golfer Admiral Alan Shepherd, and Efrem
Zimbalist Jr.

Outstanding among the home celebs—again as people, regardless of
star quotient or golfing prowess—were, again alphabetically, actors Tim
Brooke-Taylor, Sean Connery, Tom Courtenay, Albert Finney, Jeremy
Kemp, Christopher Lee, Lance Percival, and William Roache; comedi-
ans Russ Abbott, Max Bygraves, Jasper Carrott, Peter Cook, Ronnie
Corbett, Bruce Forsyth, Dickie Henderson, Eric Sykes, and Jimmy

Tarbuck; radio/TV superstar Terry Wogan; singer Adam Faith; war hero Sir Douglas Bader; boxer Henry Cooper; jockey Steve Cauthen; soccer greats Bobby Charlton, Kenny Dalglish, Jimmy Hill, and Kevin Keegan; cricket titans Colin Cowdrey, Ted Dexter, Tom Graveney, Sir Garfield Sobers, and Freddie Truman; rugby ace Gareth Edwards; auto-racing superstars James Hunt, Nigel Mansell, and Jackie Stewart; and renowned wordsmiths Ian St. John and Michael Parkinson.

Without exception, the professionals entered into and enjoyed the spirit of the event both competitively and socially. Our American pro stars were Ben Crenshaw, Hale Irwin, Johnny Miller (three times), Arnold Palmer, Jerry Pate, Lee Trevino (the record-holder with six appearances), Tom Watson, Tom Weiskopf (twice), and Fuzzy Zoeller. Aussies Ian Baker-Finch, Roger Davis, and Greg Norman, and South Africa's Gary Player headed teams, the last named three times. Seve Ballesteros, Tony Jacklin, Sandy Lyle, Peter Oosterhuis, and Sam Torrance all played twice, with Nick Faldo and Ronan Rafferty each joining us once.

Then at the outset of what would become a distinguished TV golf-commentating career with the BBC and America's ABC Sports after his years as a top tournament player, Peter Alliss served as our ever-amiable on-camera host for the first 15 series, in addition to being cajoled into tee-ing up as a celebrity a couple of times, with Tony Jacklin taking over for the last four.

Invidious as it may seem with so many headliners aboard, memory insists I offer a special salute to two in particular.

In the hope of persuading Bing Crosby to play for us—I craved the entertainment value of his super-sweet swing and seemingly effortless low-handicap scoring as much as his musical fame—Jim Wotton and I accepted an invitation to meet with him at his home in Burlingame, California, a suburb of San Francisco. I recall being a tad nervous about the mission until, after Bing personally answered his mansion door wearing a darned cardigan sweater, with another hole begging for repair, we found him so unpretentious that the visit became a joy. Yep, he'd gotten our letter, so knew the dates, the format, and the place—Gleneagles—which he said he'd long loved for both its golf and grouse shooting. And, yep, his calendar was clear at that time, so he'd be delighted to hop over and play.

In return for a contribution to one of his charities, we also wanted to billboard the series with the Crosby name, but, despite Bing's amiableness, I remained hesitant about the request. After I'd stumbled around the subject for a minute or so, he graciously came to my rescue: "I think what you're trying to ask is if you can call it the Bing Crosby whatever, right? Well, I'd be honored, so that's just fine."

One of the least enviable tasks someone in my position with such shows has to handle is having superstars videotape scripted messages—and the longer the text, the tougher the process. Here's how Bing Crosby handled his first series introduction.

At exactly the appointed chilly early morning hour, up he showed, behatted as ever in public, amiably greeted the crew in that wonderfully syrupy voice, then turned to me.

"Okay. Script?"

Prepared to duck when he reacted to its length, I handed him a page of text—at least a couple of hundred words—but told him that, of course, it's all ready to go in the Teleprompter if that was what he preferred. Glancing at the script, he cut off my concern about its length with, "Gimme a minute," then stepped away a few paces to stand alone in the blooming heather to read through the thing. Quietly and quickly, but aloud, this he did three times. I got the impression he was trying to memorize it, but couldn't believe that was possible in so short a time.

Returning to our location, Bing handed me the paper, adjusted his gamekeeper's hat with its trademark feathered band, planted himself in the designated spot, cleared his throat, and said, "Fine. Let's go."

Puzzled, I asked if he wouldn't like, well, maybe to rehearse with the prompter a time or two…so, er, just to be sure the operator rolled at, like, the proper speed?

"Nope," said Bing. "Not necessary. And I'm hungry, no breakfast yet. So just fire up the boys."

Although concerned about how far off-text he might wander, I had no option but to raise a hand to the technicians, and off we went.

Amazingly, Bing's delivery was virtually word-perfect, meaning he'd memorized the darn thing in just three quick readings. The director was so stunned he forgot to call "Cut." Humming to himself, Bing waited while we checked video and audio quality, nodded when he got the all-clear, climbed in his golf cart, said, "Thanks, fellas. Nice and fast. Breakfast here I come," and took off.

By then, I'd worked a few hundred such tapings, some featuring super-star actors. In golfing terms, Bing Crosby had just made them all look like bumbling hackers.

"Fame is the sum of misunderstandings that accrues around a name," wrote a 19th-century Austrian poet by the name of Rainer Maria Rilke.

At the time of his appearance for us, Albert Finney was one of the world's best, busiest, and most highly acclaimed actors, but there was no misunderstanding the singularity of his personality as a famous person. He was, in a nutshell, at all times the least starlike "star" any of us involved in the shows had ever encountered.

Most striking to me was Finney's clearly genuine lack of even an iota of the self-absorption—the "me, me, me" syndrome—so innate to the bearing and behavior of the majority of super-successful and/or "cele-brated" people. Out of genuine interest, I recall asking him more than once about some element of his work, but the response was always a dis-missive wave of the hand and a turn to either a non-personal subject that had engaged his interest, or an inquiry or comment related to his ques-tioner's life or thoughts.

Those of us who came to know him that week found this depth of interest in whomever he happened to encounter, regardless of what some might call "station" in life, especially fascinating. Invariably, one com-pleted a conversation with Albert Finney with an overpowering sense that the lives, styles, and perspectives of whomever he happened to meet were vastly more interesting to him than his own. Which, of course, I quickly realized, must surely have been a major contributor to his stunning range of thespian "personalities."

Whatever the fount of that characteristic, however, it surely made the man a joy to be around.

"TICKLING UP"

The world's top golfer and three friends—Royal and Ancient member and show host Sean Connery, future two-time Masters winner Ben Crenshaw, and world-renowned singer Glen Campbell—were playing a practice round in preparation for recording a three-part BBC TV special we'd cooked up to benefit a Scottish charity, headed by Connery, titled *Jack Nicklaus at the Home of Golf.*

It was the height of summer, and the Old Course was busting at the seams, but the illustrious foursome, enjoying each other's company and chatter, were in no hurry. At the 4th hole, a golf ball rolled past them as they walked after their approach shots, then a couple more as they ambled toward their drives on number 5.

This time the four stopped and stared back. As they did so, a man mounted on a moped and clad in a uniform the color of burned-out fescue, appeared from behind a clump of gorse bushes and rode over to the celebrated group. The word "RANGER" was boldly embroidered across the front of his military-style cap. Stopping, he offered a pleasant "Good day to ye, gentlemen." One could assume he recognized at least two of the four, but, if so, he showed no sign of it.

Campbell was the first to address him.

"Hi there, Mr. Ranger," Glen said. "Listen, we're glad you showed up, because those guys behind us are hitting into us. Happened three times now. Would you mind asking them to quit?"

The ranger produced a wry smile.

"Sorry, sir," the ranger said, "but I daresun't do that. Ye see, they're just tickling ye up, because ye're playing too slowly. Speed up and they'll stop and ye'll be just foine."

With which the ranger politely tipped his cap, said with a grin, "Aye, just tickling ye up, ye see," restarted his moped, and rode slowly away, presumably in search of more tardy visitors, leaving Connery—an understanding native—chuckling, and the other three looking stunned.

I didn't have the nerve to ask Nicklaus if it was the first time he'd ever been "tickled up," but I'd have bet a fair sum that it was.

It was during that same shoot, incidentally, that Glen Campbell, following let's just say an "energetic" cocktail hour—impeccably clad from head to toe in traditional Scottish garb, including a kilt in the Campbell tartan—serenaded the Old Grey Toon with a powerful rendition of "Scotland the Brave" from a precarious perch on the edge of the roof of the Old Course Hotel overlooking the course.

The hotel manager at the time said the performance was *definitely* a first. To the best of my knowledge, it also remains a last.

No "Stars" Down Under

No country I've lived in or visited during a lot of shuttling about the planet begins to compete with America in terms of "celebrity" worship. At the opposite end of that scale, in my experience, is Australia.

I could quote many examples of our Down Under friends' antipathy to most forms of pomp and circumstance, from the taxidrivers who shame you into sitting up front with them to prove your lack of "snobbishness," to the merciless "roasting" of the then world's number-one golfer, Greg Norman, at a dinner I attended that was supposed to be honoring him, to the declaration of an Aussie corporate titan to an equivalent from California who was self-importantly throwing his weight around, "Quit that bullshit. We don't allow 'stars' down here, mate."

My favorite, though, involves the late Sir Kerry Packer, the media mogul who for many year's was Australia's wealthiest citizen, but at the same time one of the most down-to-earth people you could ever meet.

The scene was an elaborate dinner party at a Pebble Beach mansion where the late President Gerald Ford was being accommodated while playing in the AT&T Pro-Am. For whatever reason, Ford couldn't be present that evening, but two of the world's golf greats—both Americans—were among the diners, along with Packer and his wife, Roslyn.

Unsurprisingly, considering the mansion's primary guest, following the meal the talk turned to how much money—multimillions, of course—would be spent (clearly rightly to the Americans present) on Ford's memorial library, his and his family's Secret Service protection, and all the rest of the outlays accorded for life to past U.S. chieftains.

As the discussion progressed, the physically imposing Packer remained wordless, but with his expression steadily souring. When finally the talk ended, he thumped his fist on the table to gain attention, then in his deeply accented Aussie growl said, "Well, you know, it's a lot different where I come from. Hell, when we kick a prime minister out down home, we don't even give him the bus fare home."

A couple of other non-natives laughed, but most of the stunned assemblage remained shocked into silence.

fifty-two

COMING TO AMERICA

This item has nothing to do with golf *per se*, but, because it relates to my *Golf Digest* employment, and possibly offers an element of amusement, I hope you'll bear with its inclusion.

Although I'd left America at an early age with my British parents, due to a combination of the Depression and my father's career advancement, I had actually been born in the U.S.A. (yeah, okay, in Brooklyn, if you must know). However, until attempting to obtain the essential visitor's visa for my first working trip back Stateside, it hardly occurred to me that, under U.S. law, my place of birth gave me claim to Yankee-hood. After a few years in Australia, we'd moved to England—again, for Pop's work—where, despite a couple of bombing-outs, we somehow survived World War II in one of the most heavily blitzed areas south of London. Accordingly, I traveled on a British passport.

To apply for a U.S. visa in London in those days required—as surely, in this age of terrorism, it now does even more—much filling out of forms, production of identifying documents, and sitting around twiddling one's thumbs at the imposing American Embassy in Mayfair's elite Grosvenor Square. Eventually, about the time you'd twiddled so long you wanted just to forget the whole deal and go home and lie down, an official would appear and call your name, whereupon you joined he or she at a counter and—assuming appropriate godliness and wholesomeness—obtained the necessary passport stamp.

I'd submitted all the paperwork and was ensconced in the vestibule with perhaps 50 other bored-looking supplicants awaiting the call, when a guy in a security-person type uniform appeared at the entrance to a long corridor, surveyed the assemblage with a look that said he knew we were all potential suicide bombers, then, in a stentorian voice, called out, "Mr. Bowden?"

A little startled, I stood up and told him that was me, whereupon he beckoned silently with a finger, about-faced Marine-style, and began marching back down the corridor into the bowels of the embassy, clearly assuming I would follow. Wondering what crime I could possibly have committed under American law as a two-year-old, after catching up I summoned the courage to ask him where we were going and why. His response was a scowl, followed by placement of a finger to his lips and continued quick-marching. I had a sense that, if I uttered another word, he'd have me handcuffed and leg-ironed.

Eventually, we arrived at an imposing oak door with a large brass name-plate that I didn't have time to read before my guard knocked, swung the monster open without waiting for a response, and waved me in. I found myself in a handsomely appointed office with a fine view of the square, a portrait of the then-serving President Kennedy behind an enormous desk, and a large Stars and Stripes on a pole partially unfurled in a corner.

Regarding me severely over a pair of heavy horn-rims from behind the desk was a person whose slight build and distinctive facial features said that his heritage, if not his present nationality, was Asian—in other words, not quite the average all-American I was semi-expecting. When this man brusquely indicated that I should sit, I did so with alacrity in the chair facing him. Distinctly disdainfully, it seemed to me, he was lightly waving some paperwork that I assumed was mine. The expression on his face as finally he dropped it on his blotter suggested that he was about to utter a sentence of life imprisonment without possibility of parole—or maybe even the electric chair.

After regarding me cryptically for what seemed like half an hour, finally he removed his glasses, gave them a quick polish with the end of his tie, and spoke.

"I understand, Mr. Bowden," he said, "that you wish to go to the United States of America? And that, in order to do so, you have today"—tapping the offensive papers—"applied at this embassy for a visitor's visa?"

The man's accent was as American as apple pie, and this eased my confusion if not my nervousness. Immigration and naturalization, of course—either he or his folks, or maybe his folks' folks, or even his folks' folks' folks. The land of limitless opportunity was also one almost entirely populated by such Homo sapiens, right?

Anyway, I answered, "Yes, I do, very much" (almost adding, "Sir!").
His eyes narrowed.

"Where were you born, Mr. Bowden?"

"Uh, well, actually, in New York. In the borough of Brooklyn. At Prospect Park Hospital, to be precise."

From the look on his face, I half expected him to say, "How unfortunate." Instead, after a lengthy pause, he asked, "Has it never occurred to you, Mr. Bowden, that you are an American citizen?"

Uh?

"Er...Well, er...No. I suppose it hasn't, not really. That is to say, er, well...No, it never actually has."

"But your paperwork here"—the vice-consul or whatever he was tapped the sheaf again—"says you were *born* in the United States of America, Mr. Bowden."

For some strange reason, the question as to why this man appeared to care so deeply about where I'd emerged into the world still wouldn't quite go away. But I did my best.

"Well, ah, yes. But, you see, I only lived there a short time, so we naturally sort of assumed, what with my mum and dad being British, and all my uncles and aunts, and my cousin Wilfred, and...Well, that I was—"

Up shot an official hand.

"Mr. Bowden, it is my duty to inform you that any person born in America, in an American possession, on an American ship, or even flying in American air space, is, under the laws of the United States of America, an American citizen." He paused, then, raising his eyebrows and peering at me sternly over his spectacles, added, "Do I make myself clear?"

Wow! This needed a bit of thinking about, but my inquisitor was clearly awaiting an answer—and not very patiently at that.

"Er, well...Yeah, I suppose...I mean, if you say so, being who you are, then who am I to argue? But, look, I only want to go for a couple of weeks and then I'll be out of there, so—"

Up went the hand again, accompanied by an even more baleful stare over the horn-rims.

"What I just said, Mr. Bowden, is subject to certain conditions, of course. One of which is that the person involved has legally claimed his or her American citizenship before the age of 21."

I almost grinned.

"Oh, dear. Well, that lets me off the hook then—"

"And has not served in the armed forces or voted in the elections of another nation."

I *did* grin.

"Well, those two *definitely* let me off the hook. You see—"

"I take it that you are informing me, Mr. Bowden, that you *have not* claimed American citizenship before the age of 21, and that you *have* served in the armed forces and *have* voted in the elections of another nation?"

As he threw out these questions, his facial expression produced a vision of him, depending on the answers, pressing a buzzer under his desk that would bring back the Marine—or maybe a platoon of Marines—this time with AK-47s as well as the cuffs and leg-chains. And, of course, if they put the CIA or the NSA on my case, which seemed to be becoming more and more probable, the truth would surely out.

So there was no option now but to fully fess up.

"Well, it's no to the first and yes, guilty on both counts, to the other two. But you know how it is over here, the national service and stuff...like how everybody has to do it here? So, yeah, I was in the Royal Air Force for 18 months—and what a bust that was! And voting? Oh, I dunno. Probably not more than, uh, three or four times..."

There came a deep sigh, as it was surely assumed I'd voted for communist-party candidates. Then, elegant fountain-pen lifted from desk, teeth tapped, all preparing for what proved to be the crunch question: "Mr. Bowden, if you want to go to America, the bottom line is that you are going to have to be an American, because American law does not permit visas to be issued to people who are, by the intent if not the precise letter of other laws, *already* American citizens. So, Mr. Bowden, we come now to the $64,000 question. *Do you or do you not want, if there is a way you can do so despite your...well, let's call them your 'infractions'...to take up American citizenship?"*

Wow! Again—and big time.

I'd sometimes thought of myself as a little bit Aussie, but, having lived in the U.K. the longest, mostly a died-in-the-wool Limey. So this was definitely a conundrum, and particularly with an instant decision clearly expected, and, if not quickly given, surely demanded under threat of some horrendous penalty.

However, what I did know for sure was that I very much wanted to cover the PGA Championship and the Walker Cup, along with a tournament in Massachusetts I'd carefully planned to take in, not to mention talking to some important golf people I'd been fortunate to arrange to meet (including one named Palmer and another Nicklaus). Also, I suddenly had a sneaking suspicion that, under U.K. law, if push came to shove, I could somehow wangle some sort of dual nationality.

So I answered smartly, "Yes, sir!"

Which brings us to the funny part.

I went home and, in an ever-fouler mood, dug out and supplied by express mail the piles more data requested by my inquisitor, which, he had told me, would be dispatched to some great edifice in Washington—I assumed, of course, my reporting mission being so critical, in an elegant briefcase chained to a senior CIA agent's wrist on a U.S. Air Force fighter jet. And, surely, although apparently not quite that way, the stuff did arrive in America's capital pretty fast, because questions soon came back, and again were smartly answered.

After which my friend telephoned.

"Mr. Bowden," he intoned, "I am pleased to inform you that proof of your true nationality, a U.S. passport, is now ready and awaiting your collection—upon just one remaining condition. Which is that you obtain and hand to me personally, before receiving the new passport, notification from the appropriate authority stating that you have surrendered your United Kingdom passport to the British government."

Britain's Passport Office at that time was located in the Pimlico section of the borough of Westminster, the London base of most U.K. government. Soon after opening time the next morning, I dutifully took my place there in a line that led eventually to a bored-looking civil servant leaning languidly on a counter behind a small, grilled hatch.

"Yurst, mate, wot can we do fer yuh," he greeted me in the broad Cockney unique to the London East-Ender. I was less than halfway through explaining the situation when he raised a hand.

"Righto, mate, I gotcha. No bovva, no need for annuver word, 'Appens all the bleedin' time, people becomin' Septic Tanks." (Septic

Tank, I hate to inform my American readers, is Cockney rhyming slang for Yank.)

With which this member of the U.K.'s governing class took my proffered British passport and disappeared, to return a few moments later with two slips of paper, which, grinning broadly, he thrust through the grill to me. Under the Passport Office's official logo and the royal seal of the British Foreign Office, of which the P.O. is a division, I read on both sheets these identical words: "The Chief Passport Officer presents his compliments to Mr. K.H. Bowden and acknowledges receipt of his passport No. 821446, issued at the Foreign Office on July 19, 1954, which this day has been surrendered to this office."

But *two* copies? I laid them side by side on the hatch ledge and raised my eyebrows to my Cockney friend.

"Well," he said with a big grin, 'It's loik this, innit? One's for them buggers up in Grosvenor Square, and the uvver's for when you decide you don't wanna be a Septic Tank no more, an' you come back 'ere to get back the passport you jus' give us so you can be a proper Limey agin."

I still have that now ancient second slip of paper, and I still laugh out loud every time I happen across it.

fifty-three

CONNING AN
ENGLISH ROSE

And now just one more diversion from golf—the last, I promise. So, I'd sort of hit what seemed to me like the big time—become an American, hired as top editorial banana at *Golf Digest*.

Assuming, that was, I could find a way to persuade a purebred English rose—whose love of her country and most of its then relatively genteel ways exceeded that of any person I'd ever encountered—to give it all up in favor of what the British press and TV had convinced her was the Devil's playground. Which, of course, necessitated her making a first visit to the place before any decision could be finalized.

This required hard thought, and I gave it such.

Very quickly my leadoff ploy became that, under no circumstances, would we fly in through New York's JFK, where I will be kind and use only the words "gruff" and "sour" to describe the look, tone, and general demeanor of most of the uniformed people one first encounters.

Instead—and this I regarded as nothing short of a brain-wave—we would take a flight from London to Miami, so timed that we arrived in the land of the free and the home of the brave in pitch darkness. After picking up a rental car, we would then drive leisurely up the, at that late hour, relatively traffic-free Interstate 95 to the island of Palm Beach, where I would have booked an ocean-fronting suite at a small but elegant hotel.

Early the next morning, taking into account our jet-lagged early rising and Florida's balmy dawn weather, I would suggest a short stroll across to and up and down the legendary Worth Avenue, followed by breakfast on the hotel's exquisite patio, followed by an hour on the glistening white beach, followed by lunch at a "celebrity" hangout, followed by an after-noon nap, followed by dinner at the famed Ma Maison.

And, boy, did it all work out beautifully—with the unanticipated bonuses of a minor traffic-jam at a red light consisting entirely of Rolls Royces, Ferraris, Mercedes, and Jaguars as we exited Worth Avenue, then a very "proper" English maître d' at our celebrity-stuffed dinner establishment.

So, both happy and tired as we sipped a rejuvenating Ma Maison cocktail, I ventured the $64,000 question: "Well, my love, how do you feel *now* about America?"

There came an adoring (I think) smile, a slow sip of the cocktail, a gentle laying on of a hand, and finally this response: "Well, I must admit it really doesn't seem too bad at all—in fact, much better than I expected."

Unfortunately, the next morning we crossed over into West Palm Beach on the start of a long journey north, whereupon, sad to say, there was no avoiding reality.

But, all these years later, we're still together, and the dear lady swears she's finally forgiven me.

part five

REFLECTIONS

fifty-four

"To Hell with 'Em!"

One thing that never fails to get my gray matter churning when I watch a TV replay of a golf show from way back when—*Shell's Wonderful World of Golf, Big Three Golf*, etc.—is how hard the players had to whack their putts to get the ball to the cup from all but minuscule distances.

The reason, of course, was that, by present standards, even the finer putting surfaces of those times were extremely slow—sometimes more sluggish than the pace of a modern well-groomed fairway.

And the reason for that? In a nutshell, turf science and technology were still in the dark ages relative to the green speeds they have since made possible.

And the trouble with that?

Here's my take on it.

Just as the appearance of the Augusta National during the Masters sets a national standard for flawless wall-to-wall emerald green, the super-fast putting surfaces now deemed mandatory to present a "real test" have become an equally essential status symbol at the "high-end" golf club level.

Unfortunately, because the shorter even the finest strains of grass are mowed, the more stressed and disease-prone they become, this inevitably produces problems. Primary among them, maintenance costs escalate exponentially for both materials and labor, greens superintendents lose hair and sleep as they grow ever more pressured and insecure, and most players' already shaky putting abilities deteriorate even further, thereby reducing their playing pleasure.

At worst, many such super-stressed greens eventually just give up and die, requiring expensive renovation or replacement while severely disrupting play. At best, they forever teeter on the brink of expiring.

How nutty can this fetish get?

Many years ago, I played in the U.S. Senior Amateur on a New England mountain course where, at high cost and with great member pride, the greens had been specially manicured for the championship to a Stimpmeter reading of around 12 or 13—or to about twice the speed they could have been gotten when the layout was created back in the 1920s.

At the players' dinner preceding the get-go, the USGA official in charge announced that he expected everyone to get around in no more than four and a half hours, despite the fact that for the first two days the large field was attempting to qualify for the event's match-play denouement at stroke-play in three-balls.

A member of my group happened to be the one of the country's top-rated senior amateurs at the time. Starting out on a long par-5, he played a gorgeous pitch to three feet past the cup cut in the back of a severely tilted green, only to face a repeat of that shot from a good 60 yards down in the fairway after his first effort spun hard, then raced crazily back to him. Thus, after playing a shot that on a green paced to fit the terrain would have produced an almost certain birdie, he ended up with an infuriating double-bogey.

Two players withdrew after 5- and 6-putting another heavily sloped, icc-rink fast green, along with a handful who simply got tired of 3-jacking. No group finished either qualifying round in under five and a bit hours.

A few weeks later I happened to run across a renowned course architect, and recounted the saga to him.

"*Ha!*" he exploded. "You think that's bad? Well, listen to this.

"I get hired to do a private club course on some land so hilly and rocky there's just no way to produce 18 reasonably contoured greens within the budget they have. So, with more than half of 'em severely sloped, I tell the guys behind the project, 'Look, hear me carefully now. Don't ever, *ever* get those greens faster than a seven or eight on the Stimp, because, if you do, most of 'em will become unplayable.'

"Well, they all nod understandingly, but then, of course, they watch the Masters and the Open and other stuff on TV, and a year later my phone rings and its this club's president bellyaching about what a terrible job I did with their greens, and what am I going to do about fixing 'em, etcetera, etcetera.

"So I let him whine on for a bit, then I say, 'Hey, just answer me one question, will you, Mr. President? How fast are your greens on the Stimp right now?'

"'Well,' he says, 'we started out like you said, but there was a lot of complaining they weren't fast enough to be a real test, so we've done a lot of work and gotten 'em up in the 10s and 11s.'

"I was so mad I couldn't talk anymore. Just had to put the damn phone down.

"But what are you gonna do? Members act like idiots, then blame the architect or the greenkeeper. Well, I say to hell with 'em!"

fifty-five

ABSURD PENALTIES

The one department of golf in which the game's rules are applied consistently and to the letter is top championship and tournament play, which perpetrated surely the greatest irony in the game's history—not to mention, in my "take," a humongous absurdity.

The victim was one of the sweetest professional stars in golf's history, the superb Argentinean shot-maker Roberto De Vicenzo. The penalty he suffered was the most savage I ever witnessed.

It happened in the 1968 Masters when De Vicenzo signed for a par on the 71st hole where he'd actually made birdie—and made it before many thousands of spectators and swarms of cameras. But, Tommy Aaron, his playing partner, had written down "4" instead of "3" on Roberto's scorecard, and, in the excitement of the moment, De Vicenzo signed it without quintuple-checking the numbers and correcting the error. Infamously, this meant that under the rules—even though he'd shot a 65 that would have won the tournament—he was judged to have scored 66, which put him into a playoff with Bob Goalby, which Goalby won.

Indicative of Roberto's unfailing classiness, his best-remembered comment was a quiet, "What a stupid I am." Unsurprisingly, a great many others were more inclined to apply that aspersion to the rule-makers and enforcers, even though the legendary Bob Jones—a true sportsman if ever there was one, but also a stickler for the rule book—had the final say on the matter.

There have, of course, been many such heartbreakers over the centuries at or near the top of golf, but never in my time so many in a short span as occurred in the game's major championships recently. To wit:

- The then-last-round leader in the Masters was penalized 2 strokes for hitting a shot that ricocheted at high speed off a bunker lip and struck him in the chest before he could leap out of the way. He later confirmed that the pain of what many witnesses regarded as a ridiculous penalty was far greater than that inflicted by the ball. (The penalty was reduced to 1 shot for such an occurence from 2008 forward!)
- In the U.S. Women's Open, a Scottish player was penalized 2 strokes for moving a spider out of her putting line with a tee peg. If she'd used her hand or putter, no problem.
- Despite their scores being correctly recorded, a potential winner from England and a top Swedish player were disqualified from the final round of the 2003 British Open for writing their tallies on each other's scorecards. Two weeks later, the championship's operator, the Royal and Ancient Golf Club of St. Andrews, announced it was giving each player the equivalent of last-place prize money in view of the fact they'd perpetrated "an honest mistake." Better yet, this perhaps most ridiculous of all rules was later changed.
- Another twosome in that championship made the same mistake, but noticed it before signing their cards and, accordingly, redid the paperwork. In commenting that common sense and the rules of golf don't always align, one of them said: "It's like the days when you stole a loaf of bread and they strung you up. You'd think we'd gone beyond the 13th century, but I guess we haven't."
- A prominent American player in the same British Open incurred a 1-stroke penalty because his ball was moved fractionally by a 35-mph wind as he was addressing it.
- Popular Danish player Bjorn Borg would have won the claret jug in 2003 but for being penalized 2 strokes in its opening round for "testing the condition" of the sand in a bunker. What he'd actually done was slam his club into the stuff in disgust after missing a shot from it. If he'd stuck that club in the sand and leaned on it to prevent himself from falling, or impaled a rake in the sand preparatory to cleaning up the mess after hitting his shot, there would have been no penalty.

These and other rules inanities produced considerable media vitriol. My favorite among the diatribes was renowned former *Sports Illustrated* star columnist Rick Reilly's sign off: "Someday the lumps of dandruff who run golf are going to realize that they are worrying about spiders while elephants are stomping the game flat."

fifty-six

MARRIED TO THE GAME

It's certainly no secret that golf can exert tremendous pressures on marriage, with wives—it seems to me from six decades of close observation—mostly getting the short end of the stick.

Of the million-plus divorces annually in the U.S., one authority estimates that overindulgence at golf by husbands is a major contributor to between 10 and 15 percent of the breakups. Beyond that, of course, he writes about the amount of marital discord, never resulting in divorce, arising from compulsive commitment to the game.

Following are a few reported examples I've happened across over the years of how golf fanaticism broke up marriages:

- When a newlywed couple living in different states got together only on weekends because of their jobs, the husband played golf for most of the daylight hours, believing that taking his wife to dinner was "enough." The same guy played on his wedding day along with 18 holes the day his wife's divorce petition was heard in court. (Talk about brass you-know-what!)
- A couple ended up divorced because, after marrying on a tee at one of the husband's favorite golf resorts, the wife refused to renew their vows six years later at the same spot.
- A father of six was on the course when three of his kids were born.
- One guy was in such a hurry to get on with a game that he ran over his (soon to be ex-) wife with a golf cart.
- The wife of a fellow who played 300-plus rounds a year, and lied about it, made him take their dog along as a possible deterrent, but he simply left the pooch in his car while he played. The same guy owned more than 100 putters and 30 sets of irons.

- When a marriage counselor proposed that a golf fanatic quit the game entirely, the man stopped just short of assaulting the guru.

Is there an answer to such antics?

The general consensus of counselors of various stripes appears to be that, when a man becomes truly demented about golf, the wife's only hope—short of flat dumping him—is to take up the game herself and join him on the links.

Of course, that's if he'll let her—because the general consensus is also that most men really only want to play with other males.

fifty-seven

GOLF'S BATTLE
OF THE SEXES

Despite periodic efforts to even things up by state and local-authority legislation—plus, occasionally, the efforts of a few fair-minded men within the organizations themselves—I believe women golfers still tend to be treated as second-class citizens at too many private clubs.

The more macho among male players openly argue, of course, that this is simply a natural expression of the eternal conflict between the sexes, and, accordingly, there is nothing that can—or should—be done about it.

More specific reasons voiced by misogynists—but usually more quietly—is that, by taking so many shots because of their relative lack of muscle and other athletic attributes, women play too slowly, or too deliberately, or insufficiently seriously, or sometimes *too* seriously (it's true that they hole out many more six-inch putts than most men do).

A more honest way of saying all of this might be, to many male golfers, that the fairer sex simply gets in their damn way!

In which regard, however, let me here put on the record that, not long ago, a study involving secret timing of all-male and all-female foursomes at a handful of upscale private clubs indicated that the majority of women's groups play faster than most men's.

The study also indicated that women players tend to abide by the rules more often and more closely than their male equivalents (hence all those six-inch holed putts!).

And, of course, as any perspicacious and honest golf teacher will tell you, when it comes to swing form, the members of the LPGA Tour make much better models for high- and middle-handicap male golfers than the youthful, super-trained, "bomb-and-gouge" aces of today's men's circuits.

Women and the R and A

Nine entities presently make up the "rota" of British Open venues.

In Scotland, they are the Old Course of St. Andrews under the auspices of the **Royal and Ancient Golf Club**, Carnoustie Golf Club, **the Honourable Company of Edinburgh Golfers at Muirfield**, **Royal Troon Golf Club**, and the Ailsa Course at the Westin International Turnberry Resort. In England, the rota members are Royal Birkdale Golf Club, **Royal St. George's Golf Club**, **Royal Liverpool Golf Club at Hoylake**, and Royal Lytham and St. Annes Golf Club.

Those I've bold-faced—five of the nine—have always been, and adamantly remain, all-male establishments. Nevertheless, all profit handsomely in pounds sterling and prestige from staging the world's oldest golf championship.

As most readers surely know, the Royal and Ancient runs the game worldwide outside the U.S. and Mexico. This naturally involves governing the players and play of both sexes.

In 2003 the R and A finally separated its governing, rules-making, and commercial endeavors (such as organizing and operating the Open and the other British male championships) from its activities as a private club. The primary reason was to eliminate the personal liability of R and A members for legal judgments or costs against the club—as, for instance, could occur through litigation by golf equipment manufacturers unhappy with its rulings on equipment specifications.

In announcing the change, the R and A indicated that it had decided to make women eligible for "invitation" to serve its new commercially oriented arm as committee members. Previously, women could serve on R and A committees only as "international advisors," never as actual members.

Not surprisingly to me, the fact that the male-only status of the club was not changed along with the above developments provoked some aggressive criticism in more "liberal" segments of Britain's media. Among the factors raised was that being an R and A member provides valuable business contacts and other profit-potential opportunities, plus a degree of golfing and perhaps even social status. The same, of course, is true, to a slightly lesser extent, of the bold-faced British Open–hosting clubs listed above.

I find it sad to report that questions of equality between the sexes appear to have had zero impact on the lords of St. Andrews, beyond the tokenism of "inviting" women to join a committee that, bottom line, is about protecting its male-only members from financial loss.

fifty-eight

TREAT 'EM RIGHT

It has always seemed to me that being a private golf club professional—particularly at the game's more upscale establishments—is one of the toughest and least secure jobs on earth.

First off, the hours "in season" are atrocious—from dawn to dark and beyond six or even seven days a week. And then there's the other potential extreme in North America—ennui when winter weather closes everything up and your wife, kids' schooling, or bank balance don't permit escaping south.

Obsequiousness to one's supposed "betters" is obligatory, but, overdone, spawns at best disrespect and at worst oppression. Over-chumminess, on the other hand, leads to the even more serious career-threat of "not knowing one's place," perhaps even to the point—God forbid!—of "Behaving like a member."

Compared to striking a balance between these two approaches, the day-to-day grunt work—running a shop, buying and merchandizing, teaching, organizing tournaments, training and managing staff, remembering everyone's name, surviving a control-freak club president or committee chairman or manager—is child's play.

And, from what I've learned over the years, the pay usually ain't anything to write home about, either.

But, boy, do us beaters and bangers need those folk!

And so, hopefully, most of us do our best to treat 'em right.

fifty-nine

"SANDBAGGERS"

If you don't already know, a golf "sandbagger" is a person who strives to maintain an artificially high handicap in order to improve his or her chances of winning net competitions—that is, events wherein the outcome is determined by deducting the handicaps of the contestants from their gross scores.

It's estimated by golf authorities that up to 10 percent of players "sandbag" at some point in their lives. The commonest way of doing so is to "post" (report) only bad scores, rather than every score as required in the U.S. by the code, if not the actual rules, of the game. Another method is to deliberately ruin potentially good scores with a few bad holes towards the ends of rounds where little or nothing is on the line. The most blatant—and risky—way to "sandbag" is simply to add more strokes to the unimportant scorecard than were actually taken.

Because all of this is flat-out cheating, it's always made me wonder about what kind of psyche it takes for a person to obtain satisfaction from winning dishonestly. But then, I've always later decided I don't really want to see inside such people's heads.

Sadly, only blatantly obvious "sandbagging" cases occasionally lead to disqualification, and, at the private club level, only the very worst instances garner banishment from further net tournament play. And I've yet to hear of even the sickest offender being expelled from a club. Fellow-player opprobrium—and avoidance—is probably the most common punishment.

sixty

"VANITY" HANDICAPS

The opposite of "sandbagging" is cultivating a "vanity" handicap, that being a number purporting a level of skill higher than that possessed by the player. Such handicaps are obtained by posting only best or lowest scores, and/or scores lower than those actually shot.

Victims of this syndrome—although perhaps more pitiable—seem to me less reprehensible than "sandbaggers," in that they don't cheat for personal gain. Rather, they are mostly just flat-out egomaniacs and/or narcissists.

Beyond their higher-than-should-be scores, you can always identify an owner of a vanity handicap by the excuses he (these offenders are invariably male) come up with during or after play. These include some form of injury or illness, working on a new swing, not having played or practiced enough, getting used to new equipment, and, as Shakespeare might have put it, the slings and arrows of outrageous fortune in terms of the number of "bad breaks" suffered during any given round.

The best advice about such people is, of course, to avoid them like the plague, certainly as tournament partners and generally in any form of play.

Note: An eminent psychiatrist friend told me that this form of self-deception, egomania, and immaturity is frequently tolerated among recreational golfers as being just another of the "character" tics that pervade rabidly competitive and/or "success"-oriented societies like ours.

sixty-one

THE EQUALITY QUEST

As the quest for equality in all things becomes ever more activist in America, the Augusta National, as the nation's supreme bastion of golfing elitism, attracts increasing heat from what the rightist of wingers love to call "do-gooders," often led by the more liberal elements of the media.

For much of the National's existence, its membership color bar, combined with a menial-work force consisting almost entirely of African Americans, stoked reformers' anger and provided them with much of their ammo.

Exacerbating those situations, of course, was the absence of black players in the first 39 Masters, until finally the irrefutable qualification of Lee Elder in 1975, under the club's own invitation criteria, brought him into the event. Since then, of course, it has been won four times by an African American called Tiger Woods and once by a black Fijian named Vijay Singh.

Albeit reluctantly, some observers believe, the club attempted to at least slightly cool its color imbroglios by admitting African Americans to membership following the PGA Championship's 1984 racism ruckus over host club Shoal Creek's explosively publicized no-blacks membership policy. The new men, of course, although differently complected, were from the same top corporate-executive mold as Augusta National's predominantly elderly, wealthy, and intensely conservative white membership.

But other sociopolitical issues inevitably have arisen, and will continue to, short of radical changes in leadership and admission policies as the present dinosauric membership dies off.

Primary among such issues of recent times was the absence of female members, the subject of a seemingly interminable war between the club's immediate-past chairman, Hootie Johnson, and the leader of an activist women's rights organization named Martha Burke. In that encounter, increasingly vigorous lobbying of the shareholders of companies that financially support the Masters, or were run by National members, became the primary irritant to the green jackets, resulting in the club eliminating such companies' commercials from a couple of Master telecasts by paying the broadcaster the hefty sums they would have received from advertisers.

In the end, though, as in so many socially based *cause célèbres*, neither side achieved more than expelling an eventually tedious excess of hot air.

However, Augusta National and the Masters got a new chairman in 2006 in the shape of Billy Payne, the man behind the 1996 Atlanta Olympic Games, than which no sports event is more absent of racism and sexism. Accordingly, it should be interesting to see what he might eventually be able to pull off a couple of hundred miles farther south.

What got my goat most during those Hootie Johnson/Martha Burke shenanigans was the PGA Tour's excuse for staying out of them, despite the fact that its members comprise most of the Masters fields, and that, after Shoal Creek, it had ruled out membership-restricted clubs as tournament hosts. Its excuse for staying on the sideline was that, because the Masters is an event over which it has no control, it could take neither action nor a public position on the issue.

Pretty darn lame, in my view. But anything for a quiet life among friends, I guess.

sixty-two

RACISM IN GOLF

Tiger Woods may end up winning 50 major golf championships and dominate the game as no athlete has any sport before him. But, despite any inspirational impact he may have—or his ever more extensive and admirable efforts to open the game to minorities through his trusts and other good works—I'm convinced that golf's deeply entrenched resistance to ethnic diversity will defeat him, along with all other crusaders.

Why?

My reasoning is that, no matter how well schooled in golf's traditions, customs, and etiquette non-affluent members of minorities may become through programs like The First Tee, and those headed and driven by Woods, there are just too few places for the great majority of such people to regularly *play the game*, especially as they achieve adulthood.

True, there are many more public than private golf courses in the U.S. But with so many of the so-called "high-enders" increasingly charging exploitative green fees, public layouts in general have become and will remain beyond the resources of the great majority of members of minorities—not to mention a lot of working-class white folk. For instance, how often can any family man (or woman) earning the U.S. median income of around $40,000 a year afford to pay a "daily fee" of anywhere between $150 to $500?

And the private clubs?

Well, I suggest you check with a member or two regarding their willingness to welcome minority kids from poor neighborhoods to their courses, even during member-playing downtimes. They'll almost certainly fudge the phrasing of their answers, but the underlying message will still be crystal clear: no way.

Or, in short, racism will prevail as it always has in American golf until society in general achieves its demise.

And don't hold your breath over that, for sure.

sixty-three

ALL ABOUT MONEY?

Even though I've been part of the U.S. "golf industry" for more years than I care to remember, I've never suffered delusions about the underlying motive of its endless agitating for more people to play more golf. That's because it doesn't take a Ph.D. to recognize that, whatever the altruistic reasons being preached—and some are valid, admittedly—at rock-bottom the motive is simply to make more money.

Such golf-industry entities include, but are not limited to, the game's primary governing bodies; its equipment, apparel, and appurtenance makers/marketers; golf periodical and book publishing owners and operatives; professional championship and tournament promoters; golf's TV broadcasters and cable casters; golf-oriented real-estate developers and resort moguls; and pretty much every other type of pay-as-you-play or daily fee golf-facility owner.

And what puzzles me most about all this is how many established players seem to enthusiastically favor such efforts. That's because I don't see how any such person of reasonable intelligence can fail to recognize that more players inevitably result in more crowded courses and even slower rounds than our present four-to-five-hour national average—not to mention the "aggro" of getting stuck behind increasing numbers of raw beginners.

Which, in turn, surely must mean that the better the golf industry succeeds in growing the game, the less pleasurable it will become for you and me.

A selfish perspective? Unquestionably.

But is the logic disputable?

sixty-four

DREAM LIVING?

So your retirement dream is to live in a golf-oriented community—
preferably gated and otherwise tightly guarded—located somewhere
in America's south or southwest, where the sun mostly shines and golf
games and other time-passers with "our kind of people" are amply available. Ideally the course (or courses) would have been designed by a
"name" architect and be of (supposed) "championship" caliber.

Pal, you got the loot and you'll find it's *open sesame!*

That's because, beyond forking out a hundred thou or up for bond
and/or initiation fees—plus eventually dues, minimums, cart trail fees,
improvement assessments, landscaping, homeowners' association
charges, etc.—all anyone generally has to do to realize that dream is commit to buy real estate on the premises.

If you find yourself a little pushed, you might get by at the market's low
end by purchasing just a condo or a cottage-size building or lot. If you're
filthy rich, a home in the form of what have been characterized as "starter
castles" will likely get you not only instant membership but invited onto
the joint's board of governors.

The reason it's so easy—again, given the moolah—is because the
membership committees of almost all such establishments, despite the
hot air some expel about candidates' non-fiscal—i.e., social, educational,
business, golfing—qualifications, almost never turn away anyone who
can handle the tab. Which, of course, is especially true while the "developer" is still beating such committees over the head about selling out his
real estate so that he can unload the place—along with the all the woes
it's by then generated for him—to the members and trundle off to enjoy
his hard-earned millions.

However, a warning.

Anyone considering this kind of supposedly idyllic golfer's "golden years" should consider the serious—but little anticipated or discussed—threat of ennui, which both personal experience and careful observation has proved to me often sets in sooner rather than later.

High-powered, go-go businessmen in particular may suppose that nothing could be finer than to exchange the pinstripes and wing-tips for shorts and soft spikes and the freedom to play their beloved game seven days a week. In reality, a great many who try that—even should they be young enough and/or remain fit enough to withstand the physical wear and tear—sooner or later find themselves becoming excruciatingly bored with the game, as surely they would with any form of overindulgence.

I found the answer to all of the above in "unretiring" back to pounding out stuff like this on a word-processor for a few hours most days, with a strict self imposed max of three golf games a week. Others turn to part-time, usually token-pay employment. For whatever reasons—and I'll leave them to your imagination—straight low-level volunteer activity, even in the best of causes, is rare among the "gated-community" fraternity.

A few souls, unfortunately, just become even more stressed and ornery by the lifestyle limitations than when they were running a chunk of the world.

sixty-five

BEWARE POLITICS

As with religion, long experience prompts me to suggest that people possessed of strong political views living at highly "upscale" golf-oriented club/communities are best off keeping those views strictly to themselves.

The primary reason is that doing otherwise, other than perhaps occasionally in a clearly joking spirit, can produce major dissension—and the more unpleasant the stronger each person's beliefs. For instance, at one South Florida development, its most rabid righty likes to describe the club's handful of lefties as "pinko liberal commies," while the lefties' favorite depiction is "greedy, selfish me-firsters." Neither, of course, make for all-around bonhomie.

Of course, the great majority of members/residents will possess the good sense generally to shun discussing politics. However, especially at social events following liberal consumption of alcohol by both sides, zealotry among a few can breed extremely unpleasant atmospheres and relationships.

Another reason to clam up on the subject is the same as that underpinning discourse at all levels of society: regardless of the strength or tenor of viewpoint and/or argument, neither side is going to truly listen to the other's, and, even if it did, will never change its irrevocably made-up mind.

However, if your love of golf, now or in the future, makes you part of such a scene, and you actually enjoy disputation, becoming any kind of honorary official, from lowly committee member on up to president, usually ensures an ample supply on a vast and endless array of near-to-hand topics.

The even better news is that all of them will be of extremely minor consequence in relation to real life—that is, compared to curing cancer, war in the Middle East, or even finding a decent putting stroke.

sixty-six

GOLF CLUB DISCIPLINE

Tales are told among golf's cognoscenti about a one-time not-so-benevolent dictator of America's so often number-one-ranked private club, the strictly stag Pine Valley, ejecting major corporate moguls from its famed course, and even from membership, for what most people would consider minor transgressions of its—or, perhaps more aptly, *his*—rules.

Augusta National, under the long Stalinist-style command of cofounder Clifford Roberts, was in the same league. A succeeding chairman of both the club and the Masters Tournament once told me that he was always on tenterhooks behavior-wise any time Roberts was within seeing or hearing range of him.

"The system here," this eminent financial man and fine golfer explained, "is to divide the annual operating expenses by the number of members, then send each a proportionate bill. I was always scared that when the bill arrived, it would be too hefty for me to afford. But I was even more scared of *not* getting the damn thing, because that meant I was no longer a member, due to having pissed off Cliff. And the worst part, for those so excommunicated, was that they were never given and very rarely learned the reason for it."

Committees at lesser establishments rarely have the guts—or the financial resources—to so harshly discipline their flocks, even in cases of truly appalling behavior.

For instance, at a theoretically highly respectable New England club, a drunken member who threw another through a dining room window after an argument received only a "naughty, naughty" letter from the board. Same with a regular inebriate who once knocked a fellow member out in the crowded bar over some imagined slight. Same, too, with a guy caught in an extremely embarrassing condition/position late at night in a locker room with a woman member, not his wife, again following over-servings of their respective favorite libations.

Inevitably, lack of disciplinary action peaks in clubs with a real-estate connection—the "high end" primary and/or secondary home developments built around golf courses just discussed. After all, how fast and furious the lawsuit would be if any such place attempted to toss out the purchaser of a multimillion-dollar home, or even take away his playing privileges for a few days or weeks! As they say in New York, "Fuggedaboudit!"

That type of situation, of course, is the primary reason the majority of America's most esteemed golf clubs—places like Winged Foot, Cypress Point, and Seminole spring to mind as prime examples, along with Pine Valley and the Augusta National—never become enmeshed in real estate.

The *really* intriguing thing to me, however, is how many golfers would give an arm or leg to become members of such establishments.

Elitism is the primary stimulus, of course, but—with men like Roberts in command—there's got to be a touch of masochism in there, too.

sixty-seven

CARTS

Across most of the planet, golf remains as it began six or so centuries ago—primarily a walking game. In America, in the 21st century, it has become at least 95 percent a cart-riding game.

Why so? To my mind, there are several reasons.

High among them is that, in a country where something like 75 percent of the population is either substantially overweight or flat-out obese, an awful lot of people are physically incapable of walking the four to five miles required by a round of golf on a full-size course without risking a heart attack or some other form of serious indisposition. Or, as an amusingly cynical golf equipment executive once described the market to his sales staff in my presence, "It's a game of OFRWGs—old, fat, rich, white guys."

Another reason so many U.S. golfers prefer to flit about on wheels is the decline of the caddie—perhaps primarily because most of today's country-club kids are too busy with other stuff to haul clubs, or simply have no need nor incentive to earn money.

But to me the primary reason for the cart invasion is, beyond question, the almighty dollar.

At all levels of the game, but particularly at pay-as-you-play establishments, from munis to five-star resorts, golf cart rentals contribute significantly to the bottom line.

Or, as a famous personage once famously stated, "The business of America is business."

sixty-eight

MASTERS COURSE
BAD FOR GOLF?

Cosmetically, no course on earth glitters and glows more spectacularly than that of the Augusta National Golf Club come the Masters Tournament each spring.

The flawless grooming of the course—indeed, of the club's entire grounds—is, of course, made possible by the immense profits from the tournament, the first and most glamorous of golf's four annual major championships. No numbers are ever officially disclosed regarding Augusta National or Masters finances, but the informed guesstimate of course-care authorities is that the National annually spends around $4 million on basic maintenance plus Masters fine-tuning—or three to four times the average first-class country club's expenditure.

Whatever the cost, through television, if not for most in the flesh, a now legendary combination of perfectionism, cash, and sweat provides golf's most stunning visual feast each April for fans of the game worldwide.

There is, however, a little-articulated downside to such meticulous and expensive manicuring: namely, its nasty impact on the pocketbooks of members of less wealthy clubs who come to believe that anything less than Augusta National grooming standards suggests inferiority in either or both playing conditions and the cosmetic niceties at their tracks. And, of course, that problem becomes exacerbated when super-status-conscious members come to regard any supposed conditioning "inferiority" as diminishing them in the eyes of their guests.

So, is the no-expense-spared conditioning of the Augusta National a bad example for golf in the broadest everyman sense?

Well, years ago over dinner one evening I suggested to a late Augusta National and Masters chairman that his course, in terms of escalating maintenance expenditures and grooming extravagances, had done more harm to American golf than any other. His immediate reaction was to get so angry that he almost choked on the chunk of steak he was chewing. Then, after a few moments of considering my conjection, he uttered the stunning words, "You know, much as I hate to admit it, I think that's probably right."

Of course, that admission didn't change anything down in deepest Georgia. Nor will it—there or elsewhere—short of much tougher governmental restrictions on water and chemical utilization for affluent grown-ups' playgrounds. However, some environmentalists—plus, I'm told, an increasing number of national and local politicians—believe those to be not only long overdue but gradually on their way.

Even if that's true and fairly imminent, I doubt I'll be around long enough to see the Masters contested over fairways and greens the color and texture of St. Andrews' Old Course's following a six-month drought!

sixty-nine

OVERBOARD U.S. OPEN SETUPS — BORING!

B etween 1979 and 2005, all but four U.S. Opens were won with under-par scores, ranging from minus 1 to the record of minus 8, with an average of minus 3.7 for those 23 championships. The other four winners over that period shot even par.

In 2006 at Winged Foot, Australian Geoff Ogilvy's winning Open score was 5 over par. Forty-nine of the 63 players who made the cut there finished in *double digits* over par, the last six of them scoring from plus 21 to plus 25 for the four rounds. Only 12 golfers all week beat the par of 70, 10 by 1 stroke, two by 2. The world's best player, Tiger Woods, missed the cut.

The more I've thought about various aspects of golf, the more strongly I've come to believe that the only rational reason for the existence of top professional tournament play is as a form of public entertainment. That viewpoint is strengthened by the fact that nowhere have I been able to find it carved in stone, or cast in bronze, or inscribed on parchment, that pro-viding a lucrative occupation for those few hundred of the world's citizens super-skilled at hitting a small white ball around a big green field justified the existence of the planet's pro tours—or even its major championships.

The American Heritage Dictionary publishes five definitions of the word "entertainment." To me the most apposite reads: "Something that amuses, pleases, or diverts, especially a performance or show."

Well, upon being confined to four long days of TV viewing of the 2006 Open by injury, not until Phil Mickelson's cartoonishly crazy final-hole fold did I become more than momentarily "amused, pleased, or diverted." Rather, for hour after hour, I remained mostly bored silly by watching the world's best golfers play the game the way my pals and I do most of the time—like choppers.

That this happened was not, of course, due to some mysterious affliction producing a mass and massive decline in the field's skills. As the thing dragged interminably on, to me all of the hunting and bunting from the newly instituted and most venomous "third cut" rough, the hacking and thwacking from its marginally less evil neighbors, the dithering, withering, and slithering on and around the bony putting surfaces, were the product of just one word: overkill.

In that it has been responsible for controlling and staging the Open since its origin in 1895, accountability—or, in my case, blame—for that situation can only go to the otherwise highly admirable United States Golf Association.

Topping the list of the various factors I believe are responsible for the Association turning its chief event into a drag is its seemingly ever-growing determination that what its principals surely regard as the world's premier championship must, regardless of any other factor, annually win the title of most brutish test of golf on Planet Earth. And—especially in the face of ever better equipment plus greater player athleticism and financial incentive—the only way to assure that, the USGA clearly believes, is by distorting the severity of the conditions under which the game is played 99.99 percent of the time. Or, to put it more bluntly, by edging those conditions to within a whisker of unplayability.

Cases in point?

I could itemize many, but will hold at three: the unputtable 18th green pin position at the Olympic Club in 1998 that cost the late Payne Stewart a second Open, the unreachable par-4 fairway for much of the field at Bethpage Park in the 2002 championship, and the unholdable condition of a number of Shinnecock Hills's normally superlative greens in 2004.

In defense of this toughest-at-all-costs phenomenon—or, at least, its so often tedious outcome for Open spectators—I could quote numerous statements by USGA Executive Committee members and senior staffers, but will limit myself to two.

Perhaps the most frequently uttered over recent years has been, "Preserving the sanctity of par," particularly by the older breed of blue blazers. Because no one—including its utterers—has been able to explain to me exactly what it means, I have always registered the phrase as nothing more than an inanity, a cliché, or both.

As for the second hold-the-fort statement—"The first priority is to identify a champion"—I could not agree more. But what I don't and never will concur with the USGA about is that the *scores* of that champion must be kept artificially high, relative to most if not all other topflight golf competition, by toughening playing conditions to a point where: (1) they are out of sync with most if not all other tournament setups; and (2) they severely inhibit the championship's entertainment value for spectators.

And especially not when a glance at the record book informs that today's Open four-round record of 8 under par is 56 *strokes* better than the score of the championship's first four-round winner a little over a century ago.

Or, in other words, that the improvements in sporting performance standards that invariably and inevitably accompany the passage of time must, if only in America's premier golf championship, for some inexplicable reason be artificially restricted.

And especially not if so doing makes what should be the world's most "amusing, pleasing, and diverting" golf show anything but.

Note: This item first appeared, in slightly different form, in an issue of The Majors of Golf, *of which I am editorial director.*

seventy

TOUR GOLF'S
DARKER SIDES

And here's more on the matter of play-for-pay golf as entertainment. Getting to know so many of the game's top pros over the years as people rather than performers, it became clear to me that—if only well below the surface in some cases—they were as multifaceted as any other group of comparable size.

And yet the fact is inescapable to any longtime tour observer/analyst that the intensely solo and selfish nature of golf, especially as played at the tour level, plus the riches available, produces or exacerbates some unappealing "surface" traits.

Tops in my experience is a mighty ego—you don't figure you can become one of the best golfers in the world without a huge amount of self-belief. Next, closely tied to the ego factor, comes extreme self-absorption, with, generally, the bigger the "name," the worse the infection. A form of semi-roboticism in the arena is another characteristic, particularly in regard to fan reaction and other forms of attention, serving in most cases as protection against loss of or diminished "focus." An overdeveloped sense of entitlement is a third, deriving surely from fawning acolytes and insane monetary rewards for mediocre performance. Bad temper exhibited physically and/or verbally is another. Inaccessibility to a media without which this version of the game, if it existed at all, would do so much more leanly surely makes the list. And I have numerous friends among my fellow "ink-stained wretches" who would gladly extend it.

Spend enough time around the PGA Tour in particular and it becomes clear that a primary contributor to such failings and foibles is overboard adulation, indulgement, and fawning—and particularly that of golf-besotted corporate moguls seeking to create or preserve friendships with the game's "stars."

Contributing also are the ever-growing amenities and services provided by tournament sponsors and/or officials. These routinely include— but are far from limited to—new top-of-the-line courtesy cars at every stop, lavish facilities for and overblown pandering to players' family members, state-of-the-art workout and therapeutical facilities freely operated by experts, rigidly enforced locker room privacy with armies of "gofers" always on hand, and dawn-to-dark gratis supplies of what is generally regarded in America as "gourmet" food.

Beyond such standard tournament bennies and goodies, a golf magazine some time ago divulged what PGA Tour members then received under the heading of "Corporate Marketing Player Benefits."

Included were a free, 1,000-minute-per-month digital wireless service package, including a phone with no long-distance roaming charges; 16 free one-way airport trips annually from an international chauffeuring service; a top-of-the-line laptop computer with custom-designed software; 20 percent off a major airline's published fares for players and immediate family members; a 25 percent discount on a major manufacturer's home and garden maintenance merchandise; half off the suggested retail price of a renowned line of watches; a hand-held computer organizer with wireless Internet service; 25 percent off all merchandise, excluding golf equipment, at PGA Tour airport shops; and, from a leading hotel chain, 49 nights of free accommodation per year, plus automatic room upgrades, check-cashing privileges, late check-out times, and complimentary newspapers.

Perhaps most intriguingly, the opening page of the booklet detailing this bonanza contained the statement: "The information in this booklet is for the players and is strictly confidential. We request that you not share the details of these benefits with anyone who is not a Tour staff member or player."

Which makes one wonder: who on high is secretly ashamed of such often totally unearned bounteousness?

seventy-one

"TEAM SPIRIT"

For most of the American professional tournament game's existence, its participants were forced by the geographical span and financial circumscriptions of their labors to be in some senses tremendously self-sufficient, while in others dedicated team players.

As the primary example of the former, all-time great Ben Hogan was famed for "digging it out of the dirt" strictly unaccompanied and unassisted, and would surely have driven any modern swing guru or mind-mender who came within yapping distance of him on a practice tee into swift and red-faced retreat with simply the iciness of his glare.

However, at the same time even a supreme loner like Hogan had—at least early in his career—little option but to be a team player by sharing with contemporaries the long, hot, boring, tournament-to-tournament car rides on inferior roads, followed by the cheap motels and greasy-spoons, that were essential to saving on expenses at a time when first-place prize money rarely approached today's last-place number. And, occasionally at least, even Hogan would share the almost universal apres-golf locker room or bar or dinner table conviviality that softened the harshness of the lifestyle while also stoking its camaraderie.

But, oh my, how things have changed!

Today's top performers increasingly surround themselves with entourages, memberships of such groups frequently including the crews of their private jets, their agents and/or moneymanagers, their caddies, their swing doctors and mind-menders, supplemented at times by trainers, therapists, nutritionists, equipment-maker executives and/or technicians, course-design associates, and even PR personages. Then, of course, there are their family members plus their retainers, along with assorted mixtures of friends and, almost inevitably, hangers-on. Accordingly, any off-hours socializing occurs largely within that "team" and/or "family" unit.

Although Phil Mickelson's retinue was unusual in the recent past for including both a full swing and a short-game teacher, today's most elite entourage, of course, is what's come to be known as "Team Tiger." But at least the world's number one player—an intensely private individual—has the grace to keep its members largely in the background, and also strictly mum on his activities and theirs on his behalf—under, one understands, threat of summary expulsion.

The primary factor underpinning this change, of course, is money— the huge amounts winnable even by also-rans compared to a few decades ago, and the resulting affordability of the clannish on-the-road lifestyles such handsome checks underwrite, with private jet travel topping the list.

To golf writers, this change has produced a huge downside, that being the ever-increasing inaccessibility of the players as personalities rather than performers.

To America's golf fans, perhaps the biggest downer is the country's ever-worsening Ryder Cup record against European players (winners five times out of the last six encounters), the multinational cultures of whose tour still breed immense camaraderie through forced togetherness, plus often a high degree of interdependence.

Or, as my high-school golf coach liked to put it, "team spirit."

seventy-two
MEDIA MAULING

The greater their success, the more wary virtually all of today's top tournament golfers become of the media assigned to cover them. This inevitably exacerbates the emptiness and/or blandness of their utterings, and thus a great many of the "quotes" attributed to them in the public prints.

As an old-school journalist, I find their caution boring and frustrating, but at the same time understandable.

Over recent years, scandal, exposure, and controversy have become the bread-and-butter of "popular" journalism, and supremely so in professional sports. Moral turpitude in all of its many forms by star athletes makes for the most "grabbing" headlines and "hottest" copy, and particularly when it extends—as increasingly it seems to—to outright criminality. Beyond those factors, however—and in this regard golf remains the "cleanest" of the top sports—almost any notable performer's opinion or viewpoint, beyond the routine or noncommittal, risks being twisted into erroneous, exaggerated, hurtful, and sometimes even career-damaging contentiousness by certain elements of the media.

Masters and British Open champion Mark O'Meara, reacting to the overlong media blitzing of Vijay Singh following the Fijian's "She-doesn't-belong-out-here" comment about the world's leading woman golfer, Annika Sorenstam, playing in the Colonial PGA Tour event a few years back, summed up the situation cogently: "The problem is this: the media wants players to voice opinions. But, if they do, not everyone is going to agree with them. Vijay made an honest statement, told us how he really felt, but he got pounded in the media for it. Why?"

The primary answer to that question is the most obvious: publishers' incessant pursuit of increased sales, leading to greater profit, through what old hands once called "dirt dishing." Also contributing to sensationalism is the decline of athlete hero worship through the recognition, by both the modern media and much of its audience, that righteousness beyond the arena does not automatically accompany excellence within it—in fact, ever more frequently the opposite.

A third factor is that, for most of golf's history, those who covered the game as specialists wrote primarily about how it had been played in shot-making terms, which information could only be obtained by walking with and watching the performers. Today's extensive television coverage, instant electronic scoring feeds, and mass post-round interviews of stand-outs, have made live-action observation by the media a labor of love, occasionally indulged in by old hands who are often tended to be viewed as cranks by their desk-bound younger peers. Which, of course, leaves the latter more time and energy for gossip and scandal.

Journalists' rapport with players has also changed dramatically as the media has grown numerically and in aggressiveness of approach.

The relationships developed by veteran golf writers with previous generations of tour regulars included levels of friendship and degrees of trust unknown today, and particularly in terms of the confidentiality of conversations occurring "off the record," as, for instance, during a plane ride or over a dinner table.

Without having to say so, a Sam Snead or an Arnold Palmer or a Jack Nicklaus knew that possibly controversial observations or flip asides made during such social interchanges would never make the next day's sports headlines. Few modern players feel they can trust the majority of today's writers that far. Outspokenness risks controversy and opprobrium; circumspection keeps things bland but peaceful.

Today's leader at speaking pleasantly and articulately at mass-media sessions—practically the only time he'll talk to writers, excepting those serving publications to which he's contracted—but without saying anything of substance, is by far and away Tiger Woods. His initial schooling in this art apparently drew from his father's skills as a military information officer, was honed by Tiger's time at Stanford, and is impenetrably underlain by an intensely private nature.

NBC Sports golf analyst and interview specialist Jimmy Roberts cogently summarized the Woods approach in a magazine article: "Look at Tiger. His every move in public is scrutinized and rehashed. His response has been to say not much of anything. The world's best golfer may be the world's worst interview. And that's the way it has to be. Woods constantly comes off as bland because there's no upside to him in being outspoken."

seventy-three

"LIP-FLAP"

With only a few exceptions, golf tournament television commentators take the opposite approach to the often controversy-seeking print media. Listen carefully and what will strike you most in TV golf-coverage talk is repetitiveness, platitudinous, blandness, and a predilection for clichés—as in, "He's got plenty of green to work with," or, "He's short-sided himself here," or, "If he can get to the house in [whatever] he's got a real good chance of winning." Or, in short, what throughout the broadcast industry is derogatorily known as "lip-flap."

One reason for this situation is the tardiness and mundaneness of much of tournament golf's so-called "action" in a medium where "dead air" is a sin worse than grand larceny. In that environment, fear of saying nothing when—as is so often the case in televising so slow and ultra-deliberate a game as golf—nothing is worth saying, trumps fearfulness of uttering inanities and banalities.

Another reason for the generally indifferent audio output is the limited vocabularies and command of the language of some of the fully or partially retired players who provide much of what's known in the business as "color" or "analysis."

Yet another contributing factor is lack of knowledge of the finer points of golf by "stars" at broadcasting other sports, assigned to work golf telecasts by network executives attempting to derive greater value for such on-air talent's generally immense earnings.

Perhaps the primary vocal tedium generator, however, is the unwillingness of most announcers and analysts to criticize players or plays, due primarily to their desire—and, in terms of access, need—to remain pally with them.

America's major exception to all of this is, of course, Johnny Miller, a former U.S. and British Open champion, who in a now multiyear announcing career has appeared never to give a hoot about player reaction to his observations, and who therefore can be brutally as well as amusingly honest in his analysis and evaluations of their efforts.

This makes him, of course, as I opined earlier, by far the best "color" man in the business, but also highly unpopular with a large proportion of players.

seventy-four

GOLFER SPEAK

M ost modern American tour pros have attended college but generally as a means of honing their games in preparation for professionalism, rather than to exert themselves cerebrally in classrooms and thereafter. Accordingly, with a few notable exceptions, sophisticated command of language is no more a characteristic of professional tournament golf than it is of other big-time sports.

My all-time favorite tour player cliché — admittedly, often delivered in response to a mindless interview question — is: "If I drive it in the fairway, knock it on the green, and putt great, I'll shoot a good score."

Beyond such inanities, another irritant to lovers of the language is the frequent misuse of words, as in, "I hit it good but putted terrible," rather than the correct — or, at least, more enlightened — "I hit it well but putted terribly."

Verbal crutches also hinder some players' ability to express themselves fluently, ranging from the repeated "uhs" and "ahs" of people required to talk who have never really mastered that ability, to the barrages of "yu' knows" of the more intellectually challenged. All we need is a sprinkling of high-school-level "I was, *like*,…" or "It was, *like*,…" to completely savage any literati's eardrums.

As just mentioned, however, a primary exception to all of this is Tiger Woods, who seems virtually bereft of verbal glitches, enjoys and employs an excellent vocabulary, and mostly exhibits excellent syntactical dexterity, even though, most of the time, his utterances remain largely substance-free.

Speaking well without saying anything is an art form in itself, and many in the media regard Woods today as its all-time sports-world master.

seventy-five

THE JOYS OF
"SPECTATING"

Watching tournament golf—or any golf, come to that—has been described by non-playing friends of mine as like watching paint dry or water boil. After attending more tournaments than I care to remember—even though mostly with easy-access-providing media credentials and work to do—I understand where they're coming from.

Compared to observing most other faster-moving sports, golf-spectating can, indeed, be quite a challenge.

First, fans have to get to the environs of the event, which, the more important it is, invariably the snarlier the traffic involved. Rarely permitted to park on the tournament course's actual premises for lack of space, they are directed into some distant field or loaned parking lot, from where reaching the action will involve either a tedious and overcrowded shuttle-bus ride, a lengthy walk, or both.

At the courses, perambulating great distances over sometimes arduous terrain, combating crowds to catch glimpses of star players, using generally rudimentary toilet facilities, standing in line for often overpriced and/or ill-prepared sustenance, and protecting oneself from the elements—wind, rain, and, worst of all, killer lightning—are all part of the "fun."

Once all that's over, it's back to the shuttles, the soggy field or distant parking lot, and more homeward-bound traffic chaos.

The fans whose courage and stamina I admire the most are the ones who take their very young children along. If I had a 10-spot for every daddy—and quite a few mommies—I've seen carrying their frequently sound-asleep offspring over hill and dale, I wouldn't be writing this book.

Is it the game, or all the fresh air, that sends those little ones to bye-byes?

Whatever, as the PGA Tour likes to stress in its advertising, "These Guys Are Good," which presumably means they are worth sizable effort to watch in the flesh.

So, as the cliché goes, have a nice day!

seventy-six

EQUIPMENT COST
AND CONFUSION

With a few billion dollars at stake annually, few industries are more competitive than the producers of golf equipment. This has led to two phenomena. One is the evolution of a world within a world. The other is ever-increasing consumer confusion.

The world within a world exists at most professional tour events, where, at least from each Monday through Wednesday, golf equipment company representatives—often supported by trailers the interiors of which resemble mini-engineering plants—throng the driving ranges and other practice facilities. Their primary business is to persuade especially the better known and/or up-and-coming players to check out their employers' latest wares. Their secondary responsibility, when players are already on staff—sometimes for huge amounts in endorsement fees—is to assist them in constantly fine-tuning clubs to fit their individual idiosyncrasies, thereby, it's hoped, minimizing the chances of them either playing poorly or absconding to some rival outfit.

Because most pros are so knowledgeable—and finicky—about their clubs, great toil and tact must be exerted in all such endeavors to keep them content. For instance, most of today's trailer tech operatives, once given a set of specs, can create or rebuild a driver in a matter of minutes. And, of course, among the companies' sales/PR team members, there are no limits on handing out freebies for trial or experimentation.

The primary objective of all this activity is, of course, purely promotional, with its cost being built into the price of the goods, thereby at least partially explaining why today's "top-end" equipment can be so expensive. As everyone within the industry knows, the price of the raw materials and/or individual components of even the finest equipment is miniscule, relative to their makers' marketing, advertising, endorsement, and other sales-incentivizing expenditures. Which, of course, is true of pretty much all consumer-product businesses.

For many recreational golfers, however, two factors beyond expense become ever higher hurdles in deciding what to play. Leading off is the confusion created by the frequency with which supposedly "new and improved" equipment is nowadays launched. Its close runner-up is the seemingly ever-increasing amount of technological gobbledygook and extravagant performance claims made for so many items.

Indeed, this has reached a point where, for most consumers lacking an engineering Ph.D. and/or a plus-handicap, strolling around a large off-course golf store, or even a heavily stocked "green grass" pro shop, trying to decide what will work best for them, is almost guaranteed to produce a migraine.

And the solution?

If there is one, it may lie in some observations by Wally Uhlein, chief executive of the parent company of one of the world's leading ball, club, and footwear manufactures, talking about what many believe to be a long-overdue equipment industry shakeout: "It's Economics 101, and a commingling of several issues. We [the manufacturers] have excess capacity and falling demand. Throw in geopolitical instability, economic recession, significant drops in the number of rounds played, the fact that the game is not growing, regulatory pressures, and compressed [profit] margins, and there is little wonder that people [in the industry] are having serious problems. Consolidation is a by-product of all those factors, and the only way out of the forest for many is to link up with someone else. Otherwise, they die."

A very smart man, Mr. Uhlein is, of course, right. But I still remain tickled by the answer to oversupply and excessive choice expressed by a golf pro from the hickory-shaft era when technological advances first began to seriously impact the game: "If you can play golf, you can play it with a shovel and a rake. If you can't, no amount of 'technology' is going to change that."

seventy-seven

BOMB AND GOUGING
VERSUS
POWDER-PUFFING

Not all that long ago, players on the PGA Tour who drove the ball between 270 and 280 yards were considered "bombers." Today, anyone who can't whale a tee shot 300 yards-plus in optimum conditions ranks as a powder-puffer.

An ongoing debate at many levels of golf is fueled by this situation, in which three concerns predominate:

1. The threat of turning many of the great older—and even some newer—championship courses, that either don't possess extra land for lengthening or can't find and/or afford more, into, at the tour pro level, outdated pitch-and-putt layouts.

2. The escalating cost of building and then maintaining ever longer and more difficult new courses, at a time when the expense of the game for the average Joe and Jenny is regarded as a primary factor behind a steadily ongoing decline in both number of players and rounds played.

3. The boredom quotient of watching top tournament play when more and more par-5 and long par-4 greens are within range of a drive and short-iron, even from most places off the fairways. "Bomb and gouge" has become the tour vernacular for this phenomenon, and, much as it elevates the income of the howitzers, more thoughtful players see it as a threat to hard-core fan interest through its diminution of the need for the game's traditional strategical and shot-making skills.

The three factors generally regarded as contributing most heavily to the advent of bomb and gouge include the ever-growing incentive of ever-rising tournament purses; better and better course conditioning, particularly in the U.S.; and the increased athleticism of tour pros, who, stimulated by the example of a "ripped" Tiger Woods, increasingly train for golf like top performers must for the overtly more athletic sports.

To many authorities, however, the big-daddy factor behind the mighty hitting is the distance capability of 21st-century golf balls.

In that regard, increasingly for years now various solutions have been proposed and debated—and surely will continue to be until some form of resolution is achieved. Of them, the most sensible to many people is creating and mandating shorter-traveling balls—by, say, 8 to 10 percent—for championship and top tournament play, while allowing purely recreational golfers to continue to enjoy the hottest missiles they can lay their hands on.

So far, however, the issue has produced huge amounts of hot air and virtually zero substantive action by the game's leading authorities.

Why?

Numerous reasons are debated wherever golf "experts" gather, but the primary two are crystal clear to anyone who understands capitalism—in this case, as exemplified by the attitude of the golf-equipment industry.

The manufacturers aren't stupid: almost since the game's origins they have recognized and heavily exploited the fact that no other factor comes close to distance potential in selling balls to run-of-the-mill players. Accordingly, no ball-maker I've talked to—which is virtually all of them—wants to be placed in a position whereby they face decreased profits by being prohibited from pitching, as major elements of their consumer advertising and marketing, how far tour professionals hit their missiles.

That's just one money factor. The other is equally intractable.

Legislating golf club and ball specifications rests with two organizations who strive for, and presently enjoy, uniformity in almost all matters pertaining to the rules of golf and its equipment. They are, of course, controlling the game in America and Mexico, the United States Golf Association; and, in the rest of the world, the Royal and Ancient Golf Club of St. Andrews.

So okay, you ask, if a few hundred pros' power is hurting golf as much as a group of influential people in the game argue ever more loudly—led, incidentally, by Jack Nicklaus—why haven't those two supposedly all-powerful entities simply upped and legislated a shorter-traveling ball for use in major competition?

The answer is that such action would almost certainly trigger instant manufacturer lawsuits against either or both of golf's rulers, which, if lost, could cost them hugely—perhaps even enough to put them out of business.

Is *any* solution to this conundrum in sight?

One possibility—although still remote, according to the club's leadership at the time of writing, is that the Augusta National mandatorily impose a reduced-distance ball for Masters tournament contestants. ("Just grab yourself a handful out of that there barrel on the 1st tee, Mr. Woods, and *bon voyage*.")

To my mind, three factors give weight to that possibility.

The first is simply that the past five or six years' lengthening and other toughening measures designed to protect par in Masters tournaments aren't working, in that winners still beat it up beyond what at least some green jackets regard as reasonable.

The second is that there appear to be no serious grounds for suit over the conditions imposed for a single event controlled by a private club on its own property, rather than a national body governing an entire sport on a rented facility (such as the USGA).

The third is that, given the prestige and short- and long-term earnings potentials of winning the year's first major, most authorities believe no Masters invitee would ever opt out, even if that meant belting a tennis ball—or even a basketball—around the famed Georgia layout.

Throughout their history, the Augusta National and the Masters have been governed pretty much single-handedly by their chairman, a position now held, as noted earlier, by William Payne, the man behind the 1996 Atlanta Olympics.

By doing the above, the possibility exists that Mr. Payne would lead the resolution of what otherwise is likely to linger on and on as golf's most intractable problem. Should he decide to give it a whirl, I for one would applaud loudly, in addition to gluing myself to a TV screen for every moment of the first go-around.

Just imagine: top contenders Tiger and Phil are paired together in the final round, whereupon the former lashes his opening tee shot a measly 280 yards. "Good drive," says the latter, before blasting one out there 285.

Now, strictly for fun, let's turn the coin over and assume that meaningful restrictions on the distance properties of golf equipment will never be imposed. In that case, tightening and otherwise toughening courses without lengthening them would be the easiest and least costly way to curb bomb and gouge.

Tightening obviously can be achieved by narrowing fairways and expanding or increasing hazards, or both, as per especially U.S. Opens (*see page 210*). Upping the acreage and severity of rough, firming fairways, hardening greens, and cutting holes more inaccessibly—think U.S. Open conditions again!—are other primary ways of stiffening the scoring challenge.

A problem with that, however, is that it again runs us into the fairness factor—that being, as long courses favor "bombers," shorter but tighter ones theoretically would throw the advantage to "powder-puffers."

And there's an even testier factor.

As discussed previously, at root top tournament golf—like all professional sports—depends for its existence solely on its "entertainment" value, which determines its degree of fan support. In which regard, extreme course tightening and toughening would also butt us up against our old friend, the almighty dollar.

That's because what turns on most golf fans, whether in the flesh or watching the game on TV, is the mighty hit, headed by colossal drives (for proof, check out super-bomber John Daly's gallery numbers, regardless of how he's scoring). And, of course, the tighter and tougher the courses, the fewer such "Ooooh!" and "Aaaah!" shots would be played—or, at least, played successfully and thus excitingly. Which leads to the question of to what degree "powder-puffing" would negatively impact gate receipts and, through TV audience size, broadcast rights fees.

Which, of course, in turn, eventually might cut players' incomes by reducing purses, not to mention the compensation packages of everyone professionally involved in staging big-time golf.

And if you think either of those last two things is ever going to happen, an appointment with your nearest psychiatrist might be a splendid idea.

Note: Anyone believing he or she has solutions to any or all of these problems, please call or write the USGA or the R and A—not me!

seventy-eight

UNIMPORTANT

The wisest words I ever read about the Ryder Cup were written by veteran sports writer and editor Walter Bingham just ahead of the 2006 match in Ireland, in an American newspaper column.

I quote their key components here:

"A number of years ago I was watching the Super Bowl in my *Sports Illustrated* office in New York—yes, we worked on Sunday—which was 20 stories up in the Time-Life Building overlooking New York's Sixth Avenue.

"During a commercial, I stood to stretch and, looking out a window, saw heavy traffic below. Not everyone in the world is interested in the big game, I realized."

Bingham went on to talk about—and to—the four neophytes on the U.S. squad, then ended:

"Now back to my Super Bowl epiphany and some advice to [Brett] Wetterich, [Zach] Johnson, [Vaughn] Taylor, and [J.J.] Henry. (Future team members might also do an ears-up.)

"Do not, repeat, *do not* think that the honor of the United States of America rests on your shoulders. What you do in Ireland is unimportant. Iraq is important. Katrina is important."

As least one of us "inky wretches" still lives in the real world.

seventy-nine

NO D-AVERAGE
GOLFERS ALLOWED

Among the most succinct and down-to-earth golf books I ever read is
It's Only a Game, by Jackie Burke Jr., one of history's most astute and
down-to-earth top tournament golfers, and, following his competitive
years, the cocreator with his late great friend, Jimmy Demaret, of
Houston's Champions Golf Club—which Jackie was still operating as
well as any club in the country in his mid-eighties.

Here's my favorite passage:

> It costs $25,000 to join Champions Golf Club. There are people who
> can afford a lot more than that, but that doesn't mean *we* can afford
> *them*.
>
> I'm talking about rich guys with high handicaps who primarily want
> to bring out guests, throw dinner parties, and show people how impor-
> tant they are. I prefer someone who can afford to get in, but who also
> has thousands of hours invested in the game. Say you paid a guy an
> hourly fee for the time he has put into golf. Add up those thousands of
> hours, and you'd owe that guy a lot of money. We get that guy and all
> he brings—his devotion, his adherence to the rules, his appreciation of
> tradition and competition—for that initiation fee. This is not the guy
> who cares more about a big dance floor than getting his clubs
> regripped. We get real golfers here, people who add to the fabric of this
> club. We go after the competitors.
>
> I liken us to Stanford University, Yale, or Harvard. They don't
> accept D students academically, and we don't accept people with a D
> average in golf.

eighty

WHY SO POPULAR

Golf may not be growing as it did for so many years in number of play-ers or rounds played in America, but, at the highest professional lev-els in its top championships and tournaments, there is no doubt that the game retains a healthy spectator appeal, despite those and the other neg-atives discussed earlier.

Accordingly, as a way of signing off on a positive note, with thanks to the unknown author, I cribbed the following from the Internet:

- Golf is an honorable game, with the overwhelming majority of play-ers being honorable people who don't need referees.
- Golfers don't have some of their players in jail every week.
- Golfers don't scratch their privates on the golf course.
- Golfers don't kick dirt on, or throw bottles at, other people.
- Professional golfers are compensated in direct proportion to how well they play.
- Golfers don't hold out for more money, or demand new contracts, because of another player's deal.
- Professional golfers don't demand that the taxpayers pay for the courses on which they play.
- When golfers make a mistake, nobody is there to cover for them or back them up.
- The PGA Tour raises more money for charity in one year than the National Football League does in two.
- You can watch the best golfers in the world up close at any tourna-ment, including the majors, all day every day for $25 or $30. The cost for a seat in the "nosebleed" section at the Super Bowl will cost around $300 or more.

- You can bring a picnic lunch to the tournament golf course, watch the best players in the world, and not spend a small fortune on food and drink. Try that at one of the taxpayer-funded baseball or football stadiums! If you bring soft drink into a ballpark, they'll give you two options—get rid of it or get out.
- In golf, you cannot fail 70 percent of the time and make millions of dollars a season like the best baseball hitters (.300 batting average) do.
- Golf doesn't change its rules to attract fans.
- Golfers have to adapt to an entirely new playing area each week.
- Golfers keep their clothes on while they are being interviewed.
- Golf doesn't have a free agency.
- In their prime, Arnold Palmer and other stars would shake your hand and say they were happy to meet you. In his prime, Jose Canseco wore T-shirts that read, "Leave Me Alone."
- You can hear birds chirping on the golf course during a tournament.
- At a golf tournament (unlike at taxpayer-funded sports stadiums and arenas) you won't hear a steady stream of four-letter words and nasty name calling while you're hoping that no one spills beer on you.
- Tiger Woods can hit a golf ball three times as far as Barry Bonds can hit a baseball.
- Golf courses don't ruin the neighborhood.

We began this book with King James IV's derogation of the connection between "goffers" and "wiski," but, if the following answer to why standard-sized courses have 18 holes is true, His Majesty's disgruntlement with the game had minimal to zero impact on players of those times.

According to this legend, during a discussion among the club membership at St. Andrews a few years later, one fine fellow pointed out that it took exactly 18 holes to polish off a fifth of Scotch. By limiting himself to only one shot of the national beverage per hole, the man figured a round of golf was finished when the bottle was emptied!

And so a full "round" became forever defined.

Cheers!

INDEX

A

Aaron, Tommy, 101–4
Abbott, Russ, 165
Ailsa Golf Course, 34, 192
Allem, Fulton, 155
Alliss, Peter, 166
Anderson, Willie, 64
Armour, Tommy, 11
Astor, Nancy, 136
Augusta National Golf Club, 5, 112,
    117–120, 121–22, 183, 197–98, 205,
    208–9, 229. *See also* Masters
    Tournament
    membership rules, 115–16
Aultman, Dick, 73
Azinger, Paul, 150–51, 154

B

Bader, Douglas, 166
Baker-Finch, Ian, 166
Ball, John, 11
Ballesteros, Severiano, 11, 49–51,
    157, 166
Bean, Andy, 153
Beman, Deane, 29
Bingham, Walter, 231

Boomer, Percy, 76–78
Borg, Bjorn, 187
Bowden, Jean, 178–79
Braid, James, 11, 58
British Open, 187
Brooke-Taylor, Tim, 165
Brooman-White, Caroline, 156
Bryant, Bart, 154
Burke, Jackie Jr., 232
Burke, Martha, 198
Bush, George H.W., 154
Bygraves, Max, 165

C

Camoroli, Craig, 154
Campbell, Glen, 157, 165, 169–70
Carner, Joanne, 157
Carnoustie Golf Club, 192
Carrott, Jasper, 165
Casper, Bill, 11, 58
Cauthen, Steve, 166
Charlton, Bobby, 166
Chirkinian, Frank, 102
Churchill, Winston, 136
Connery, Sean, 50, 130–32, 157,
    165, 169–70

Cook, Peter, 165
Cooper, Henry, 166
Corbett, Ronnie, 165
Cotton, Bill, 156
Cotton, Henry, 11, 94–95
Couples, Fred, 154
Courtenay, Tom, 165
Cowdrey, Colin, 166
Crawley, Leonard, 99–104
Crenna, Richard, 165
Crenshaw, Ben, 35, 50–51, 126, 157,
    166, 169–70
Crosby, Bing, 161–62, 165, 166–68
Cypress Point, 206

D
Dalglish, Kenny, 166
Daly, John, 153, 230
Daniel, Beth, 157
Darwin, Bernard, 3, 61, 108–11
Davis, Bill, 14, 20
Davis, Roger, 166
De Vicenzo, Roberto, 186
Demaret, Jimmy, 232
Dexter, Ted, 166
Dey, Joseph C. Jr., 145–46
Diaz, Jaime, 53
Dickinson, Gardner, 70

E
Edwards, Gareth, 166
Eisenhower, Dwight D., 119–20
Elder, Lee, 197
Els, Ernie, 154

F
Faith, Adam, 166
Faldo, Nick, 11
Falk, Peter, 165
Finney, Albert, 165, 168
Forsyth, Bruce, 166

G
Gates, Bill, 114
Gill, Howard, 16
Goalby, Bob, 186
Graveney, Tom, 166

H
Hagen, Walter, 3–4, 58, 64
Haney, Hank, 49–50, 72
Hanmer, P.W.T., 125–27
Hannigan, Frank, 118
Harmon, Butch, 72
Harris, Phil, 165
Hayes, Mark, 35
Haynie, Sandra, 157
Henderson, Dickie, 166
Hill, Jimmy, 166
Hilton, Hilton, 11
Hoch, Scott, 153
Hogan, Ben, 4, 8, 12–18, 47–48, 58,
    64, 215
    at work, 19–21
Hogan, Valerie, 12, 21
Honourable Company of Edinburgh
    Golfers at Muirfield, 125–29, 192
Hoylake. *See* Royal Liverpool Golf
    Club at Hoylake
Hunt, James, 166

I

Irwin, Hale, 11, 152, 153, 166

J

Jacklin, Tony, 166
Jacobs, John, 53, 71–72, 89
Jastrow, Terry, 33
Jenkins, Dan, 71
Johnson, Hootie, 198
Jones, Bobby, 4–5, 58, 64, 76, 117
Jones, Rick, 70

K

Keegan, Kevin, 166
Keel, Howard, 165
Kemp, Jeremy, 165

L

Langer, Bernhard, 157
Leadbetter, David, 86
Lee, Christopher, 165
Lehman, Tom, 154
Little, Sally, 157
Locke, Bobby, 11, 45–48
Longhurst, Henry, 99–104
Lopez, Nancy, 157
Loxahatchee Club, 31
Lyle, Sandy, 166

M

MacKenzie, Alister, 31
MacMurray, Fred, 165
Maltbie, Roger, 35, 152, 153
Mann, Carol, 96
Mansell, Nigel, 166

Marr, Dave, 12
Martin, Dick, 165
Masters Tournament, 5, 107, 112, 208–209. *See also* Augusta National Golf Course
penalties, 186–187
Memorial Tournament, 152–55
Mickelson, Phil, 11, 58, 210, 216
Middlecoff, Cary, 11, 71
Miller, Johnny, 11, 41–44, 157, 166, 221
Mitchell, Herman, 37
Morris, Tom Jr., 11
Morris, Tom Sr., 11
Mudd, Jodie, 153
Muirfield. *See* Honourable Co. of Edinburgh Golfers at Muirfield
My Story (Nicklaus, Bowden), 26–27

N

Nelson, Byron, 5, 52–53, 54–55, 58, 121
Nicklaus, Barbara, 21, 28, 154
Nicklaus, Jack, 6, 8, 9, 10, 26–33, 35–36, 39–40, 50–51, 58, 64, 150, 157, 169–70
and instructors, 69–70
Memorial Tournament, 152–54
and Byron Nelson, 52
and Clifford Roberts, 115–16
Norman, Greg, 11, 153, 154, 157, 166, 170

O

O'Meara, Mark, 217
Ogilvy, Geoff, 210
Olazabal, Jose Maria, 51, 64
Oosterhuis, Peter, 101, 166
Ouimet, Francis, 9

P

Packer, Kerry, 170–71
Palmer, Arnold, 6–7, 10, 13, 28, 58, 64, 95, 153, 166, 234
    and Clifford Roberts, 116
Palmer, Winnie, 154
Parkinson, Michael, 166
Pate, Jerry, 157, 166
Pavin, Corey, 150
Payne, Billy, 198, 229
Penick, Harvey, 72
Percival, Lance, 165
Pine Valley, 206
Player, Gary, 7, 8, 58, 64, 153, 166
Pleasant Valley Golf Course, 12
Presidents Putter, 109

R

R and A. *See* Royal and Ancient Golf Club of St. Andrews
Ray, Ted, 9, 76
Reilly, Rick, 188
Roache, William, 165
Roberts, Clifford, 5, 112–24, 205
Roberts, Jimmy, 218
Robertson, Allan, 11
Royal and Ancient Golf Club of St. Andrews, 147–49, 187, 192, 228
Royal Birkdale Golf Club, 192

Royal Liverpool Golf Club at Hoylake, 192
Royal Lytham and St. Annes Golf Club, 192
Royal St. George's Golf Club, 192
Royal Troon Golf Club, 192

S

Sarazen, Gene, 7–8, 54–55, 58, 64
Savic, Pandel, 31, 69–70, 154
Seitz, Nick, 18, 20
Seminole Golf Club, 206
Shady Oaks Country Club, 16, 19
Shepherd, Alan, 165
Sherman, David, 156
Shoal Creek, 197–98
Singh, Vijay, 197, 217
Smith, Alex, 64
Smith, Willie, 64
Snead, J.C., 101
Snead, Sam, 8, 56–57, 58, 64, 72, 153
Sobers, Garfield, 166
Sorenstam, Annika, 217
St. Andrews. *See* Royal and Ancient Golf Club of St. Andrews
St. John, Ian, 166
Stephenson, Jan, 157
Stewart, Jackie, 166
Stewart, Payne, 150–51, 211
Sykes, Eric, 166

T

Tarbuck, Jimmy, 166
Taylor, J.H., 11, 58
TelEvents, 156–71

Thomson, Peter, 11
Toski, Bob, 53, 73–75
Torrance, Sam, 166
Trevino, Lee, 8–9, 37–40, 49, 58, 152, 166
Truman, Freddie, 166
Turnberry. *See* Ailsa Golf Course

U
U.S. Open, 210–12, 230
Uhlein, Wally, 226
United States Golf Association, 211–12, 228

V
Vardon, Harry, 9–10, 11, 52, 58, 64, 76
Verrecchio, Kim, 86

W
Wadkins, Lanny, 51
Ward, Harvie, 109
Ward-Thomas, Pat, 105–7, 109–10
Watson, Tom, 10, 35–36, 58, 64, 126
Wethered, Joyce, 110
Whitaker, Jack, 150–51
Wind, Herbert Warren, 105, 108–111
Winged Foot, 206
Wogan, Terry, 166
Woods, Tiger, 8, 10–14, 27, 58, 60, 64, 69, 153, 154, 197, 199–200, 210, 216, 218, 228, 234
Wotton, James, 156, 166

Z
Zimbalist, Efrem Jr., 165
Zoeller, Fuzzy, 51, 166

About the Author

Of the 21 books Ken Bowden has written about golf, 12 were coauthored with Jack Nicklaus, including the worldwide all-time instructional bestseller *Golf My Way*. Prior to his near-40-year association with the Golden Bear, which also included television and home-video production, he served as the founding editor of Europe's premier magazine on the game, *Golf World*, followed by editorial directorship of America's leader in the field, *Golf Digest*.

Among others with whom he has coauthored top-selling books and/or produced videos are the British PGA Hall of Fame teacher John Jacobs and America's legendary instructor Bob Toski.

A low-handicap player for more than 50 years—from plus-1 at his best to 5 as *Teeing Off* was published—Bowden has won more than 40 club championships on both sides of the Atlantic, with a Canadian Super-Senior Championship victory his proudest achievement.

The latest recognition of Bowden's work comes from his golf-writing peers, who selected Ken as the recipient of the 2008 Memorial Tournament Journalism Award.

Ken Bowden resides with his wife, Jean, in Westport, Connecticut, and Jupiter, Florida.